Behind the Mask

Josh Piterman

Praise for *Behind the Mask*

'A brave and vulnerable reflection of an incredible onstage career, and the answers to some of life's most pressing and challenging questions.' —JELENA DOKIC

'This book will help so many people find the freedom and courage to be their true selves, offering not only wisdom but also insight into the actual work that needs to be done. Bravo Josh Piterman.' —BEN CROWE

Behind the Mask

Josh Piterman

echo
PUBLISHING

Echo Publishing
An imprint of Bonnier Books UK
6/69 Carlton Crescent
Summer Hill NSW 2130
www.echopublishing.com.au

Bonnier Books UK
HYLO, 5th Floor,
103–105 Bunhill Row
London EC1Y 8LZ
www.bonnierbooks.co.uk

Echo Publishing acknowledges the traditional custodians of Country throughout Australia. We recognise their continuing connection to land, sea and waters. We pay our respects to Elders past and present.

First published 2025

Printed and bound in Australia by Griffin Press

The paper this book is printed on is certified against the Forest Stewardship Council® Standards. Griffin Press holds FSC® chain of custody certification SGS-COC-001185. FSC® promotes environmentally responsible, socially beneficial and economically viable management of the world's forests.

Editor: Rebecca Fletcher
Page design and typesetting: transformer.com.au
Cover design: Peter Long
Cover image: Sam Tabone

A catalogue entry for this book is available from the National Library of Australia

ISBN: 9781760689735 (paperback)
ISBN: 9781760689742 (ebook)

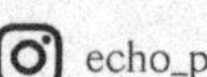
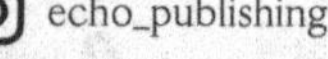

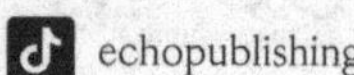

echo_publishing
echopublishingaustralia
echopublishing

For all those curious souls asking
life's bigger questions

Foreword

Far from expressions of dishonesty, the masks we wear are sacred and essential mediums in our human journey, present from our very first breath. They serve as delicate outlines of who we might become – the artist's first brushstroke on the canvas of our being. Yet, as we take on the weight of responsibility, expectation and the stories imposed upon us, they can begin to rust in place. The challenge, then, is not to reject the mask but to bring it into conscious awareness. Too often, we forget that we are not the mask itself but the pure essence of the Self, waiting patiently behind it.

Josh Piterman's *Behind the Mask* is an invitation to step into the sacred fire of unmasking, to dance with vulnerability and burn away the illusions that keep us tethered to who we think we should be. His words echo an ancient yearning, a call from the depths of the soul to awaken from the dream of pretence and return to the raw truth of who we really are. In the world of mythology, the mask often represents transformation. The shaman wears it to bridge worlds; the warrior dons it to confront the shadow. The mask represents the power of the human spirit, yet it is behind the mask where the true source of that power resides.

Josh reminds us that life itself is a ritual, a theatre of becoming where we are both performer and audience. Through his personal journey – from the grandeur of the West End to the quiet recesses of inner work – he leads us to an old understanding: the mask is not a prison but a portal.

There is something of the Phantom in all of us, hiding our wounds behind the half-mask of achievement or aesthetics. We cling to it as if our very survival depends on it, fearing that what lies beneath might be too broken, too unworthy, to be seen. However, as Josh so openly shares, it is in these dark and tender places that we find our true humanity – and our innate genius.

We are each being called to ride out and meet our own life on the back of a wounded, gammy-legged donkey, with a rip in our pants and our head held high. If we can find the courage to drop the reins it will deliver us right into the centre of our own being.

Josh never pretends the process is easy. As he descends into his own wounds, he illuminates the muddy, messy and painful work of self-discovery. His voice is a companion, a torchbearer for those willing to walk this pathless path. His honesty, humour and wisdom shine through, offering practical tools not just for reflection but for transformation.

As you read this book, may you feel the stirrings of your own courage. May you find solace in the recognition that you are enough, just as you are, unmasked and unadorned. And may you, like Josh, begin the sacred work of reclaiming the song in your heart. The world asks nothing more of you than the truth of your unmasked face.

Asher Packman, Founder of The Fifth Direction and former President of Meditation Australia

Contents

Introduction

The opening night of a musical is wild – the mad rush of adrenaline, the excitement and thrill of the crowd eagerly taking their seats, the infectious nervous energy of the cast. Then there's the pretending to have it all together, that you're not feeling the overwhelming pressure and expectation, that you're in control, when really you're shitting bricks. When performers say they love opening nights, I always want to call bullshit. I don't love them at all – they generally suck! The best I can hope for is to get through unscathed, have a relieving glass of champagne at the end and try to get some sleep if my body will allow it. Hopefully, when I wake up, the reviewers haven't crucified me.

But on 9 September 2019, at what was then known as Her Majesty's Theatre in London's West End, that changed. That was the night I publicly put on the Phantom's iconic half-mask for the first time and shared my version of the equally iconic character with an audience. Was it the perfect performance? God no. But I felt like I was flying, soaring above the theatre and the peak of the mountain I had spent my whole career trying to reach. At the same time, I felt like I had finally landed. It was one of the most exhilarating and fulfilling nights of my life. Even more special was having both my parents and my London family there.

There is nothing quite like being on stage, completely immersed in a character like the Phantom. It's utterly transcendental. Still, the feeling is visceral ... so rich, so moving, so free, if you let it be. This was the feeling I had pined for as an artist for my whole career. Sure, I'd had glimpses of it, fleeting moments, but the Phantom became like a meditation for me, a place to go into that other world, the non-ordinary world, into the heart. In those moments, it was pure magic.

I'd had big dreams ever since I started performing in musicals as a 16-year-old at high school. I fell in love with both *The Phantom of the Opera* and *Les Misérables* very quickly, and my goal was to play lead roles in both those shows, hopefully the Phantom and Jean Valjean. So that's what I did. It took me twenty years of climbing the undulating paths of the internal and external mountains to get there, but I climbed them. This was my way of being successful, of having worth, having currency, meaning something, of becoming 'somebody'.

But recently, especially as my success as a musical theatre performer has objectively expanded, I've become less interested in becoming 'somebody' and more curious in finding out who the 'nobody' is. I've begun asking questions that I'm sure you've asked yourself before – who am I without the stage lights (maybe not that one), the career, the identity I've created for myself ... or the one that has been bestowed upon me? Is this all there is to me?

I've been digging deeper into my own psychology, tapping into what lights up my heart, descending consciously into the uncharted expanses of my soul and meditating on what's buried beneath layers of conditioning. Probing what painful truths need untangling, what darkness needs illuminating. I've played many roles in my life on and offstage. I've had loads of losses and some fairly profound wins, but I've realised that external success was never going to be enough. At some point, instead of looking outward for validation, I had to look inward. I had to go behind the mask.

I wanted to work out what life is really about and how best to navigate my way through it. This book includes many of the lessons, learnings and wisdoms I found. Some I've formulated, others I've stumbled across while reading one of a plethora of philosophical, spiritual and self-help books over the years. Others are from the various coaches, teachers, gurus, guides, mentors, therapists and philosophers, alive or deceased, who have helped me grow through the ups and downs of life and self-discovery. Some have come to me through my podcast, *Behind The Mask.* My intention is not only to give you a backstage VIP tour of my world, but also to provide you with some useful tools to help you navigate your way through life, to find deeper meaning, explore a growth mindset and ensure it's all done with a touch of humour. Hopefully, that's why you're here.

If so, I suggest you have a journal handy – you'll need it.

1

PART 1

Masks

Understanding masks

To take off our mask and see what's behind it, we first have to understand what masks are and acknowledge that we're wearing them. I don't mean your *Fifty Shades of Grey* masquerade-ball situation, though I'm not knocking that either. We've all got a kink or two ... right? I'm referring to the metaphorical masks we all wear: at work, at home, with our friends, maybe even with our families. We are rarely our whole selves. Each mask is a different role: the role of the parent, partner, child, work colleague or friend. These masks remind us of who we are in this interaction and how we should act.

In Latin, the word for mask is 'persona', a part of the ego we choose to project to the outside world. It is the identity we've created for ourselves or have bestowed upon us. But there's a difference between consciously adopting masks to play necessary roles in life, and unconsciously donning masks to cover up what might be hidden underneath or to inflate our egos. People often wear masks unconsciously when they have something to hide, such as a part of themselves they don't value, trust or have full confidence in. But masks aren't the enemy, as the the roles we play in life are vital. It's about not getting trapped in those roles or our egos, and seeing our masks as a servant, not our master.

The great Hindi text *Bhagavad Gita* says, 'Do not be identified with being the actor, nor be attached with the fruits of your actions.' It's clear that our relationship with our ego dates back to ancient times. The late American spiritual teacher Ram Dass referred to this as 'somebody training'. Apparently, nobody wants to be a nobody, so we're out in the world trying to be a somebody. I'm sure you've all heard a version of this exchange:

'Did you hear about old mate? He got a lead role on the West End.'

'Oh yeah. I saw his socials. He's killing it. Good for him – he's really *somebody* now.'

Sure, old mate is doing well, and I'm pleased for him, but he was a 'somebody' well before a couple of stagey folk having a yarn about him decided he was somebody. He was also a somebody well before he wore a mask (literal or metaphorical) – and yes, I'm talking about myself in the third person.

It wasn't my West End success, achievements, bank

account or any of the masks I wore that made me somebody, because I was still somebody when I was *nobody*. And, more importantly, I was interested in finding out who the nobody was once I had become somebody.

Although we may like to think otherwise, we are the victims of somebody training – it's embedded into Western culture. This leads to harmful comparisons and the negative judgement of others. For me, it has also led to all sorts of issues around inadequacy, scarcity, shame, perfectionism, imposter syndrome and a lack of capacity for self-love.

It's a hard thing to acknowledge when we've been indoctrinated into a rigid school of thinking ... don't I know it. For me, somebody training kicked off early. It's what drove me to wear more than just the Phantom mask – the winner mask, the successful mask, the attractive mask, the charming mask, the relevance mask, the victim mask, the list goes on. For a long time, I couldn't understand how I could be anyone unless I was playing one of these roles or wearing one of these masks.

But we don't own these masks. They aren't really us – they're roles we play, not the full truth. And until we can know and love the person behind these masks, we will find ourselves chasing the next thing to be, the next mask to wear.

So, how do we take our mask off when we are afraid of being seen for what's behind it?

The first thing is to understand why we are wearing these masks. Sometimes, we are so traumatised by or afraid of what's behind the mask that, rather than taking them off, we turn to distractions and addictions: porn, alcohol, drugs, gambling, cigarettes, vapes, exercise, social media or mindless television-watching. Sometimes, masks play into our ego's desire for validation – we get compliments, praise and pay rises for wearing them, as well as love and attention, so we unconsciously keep them on.

But if these are the answers to our problems, then why are we living in a world that's more chronically discontent, dissatisfied, depressed and anxious than ever before? A world where people are lacking in meaning and purpose? Maybe it's because if we can't love what's behind the mask, then we're never going to feel full. Until we ditch the distractions and learn to love ourselves as nobodies, we will never truly love ourselves as somebodies.

To find out who that person is, we need to step behind the masks, behind the persona. We need to understand who we always were before we can realise who we might become.

Who am I?

Before I was singing on some of the world's biggest stages or taking on the iconic lead roles in *The Phantom of the Opera*, *Les Misérables* and *West Side Story*, my life felt fairly normal.

I was born on Broadway on 26 October 1985. I know what you're thinking about me, the 'musical theatre dude' – that's serendipitous, coincidental ... possibly even fate.

But don't worry, it's not the bright lights of Times Square. It's inner-Melbourne suburbia – Broadway, Camberwell – right at the top of the junction around the corner from JB Hi-Fi and Sofia's Family Restaurant, where a small bowl of bolognaise was still twice as big as my above-average-sized 4-year-old head.

I have vivid memories of my childhood on Broadway, very few of which involve singing or acting. You won't find me posting old family videos of me sporting a hairbrush microphone, fluoro bike shorts and an oversized New Kids on the Block tee, belting out showtunes in the living room like other musical theatre folk born in the '80s. That just wasn't me. I did once choreograph a version of East 17's 'It's Alright' with some friends in year 3 that we shared awkwardly in front of our classmates for show-and-tell. It was my favourite song at the time, and I'm pretty sure the whole thing was my idea, but fortunately we all moved on from that painfully embarrassing episode quickly. Other than that and reluctantly playing a security guard in the uninspired year 7 musical *Germs*, performing was nowhere near the radar.

Sport definitely was. Post-school afternoons and weekends were spent bowling and batting against a brick wall or shooting hoops in the backyard and, of course, kicking the footy around with dreams of playing for my beloved Western Bulldogs (Footscray, in those days). Mum and Dad were asked to join in for many of these episodes, but a lot of my childhood memories are of me playing sport alone, just me and my wild imagination.

Like many footy-obsessed Melbourne boys, I fantasised about playing in an AFL Grand Final. It's late in the last quarter, and we're down by five points. I'm at full forward (obviously) and I take a big pack mark on a tough angle just as the siren sounds. It's all on me. I'm lining up for the goal to win the premiership, and the weight of expectation is on my boot. The deafening silence reverberates throughout the stadium as I begin my slow, methodical approach towards the big sticks. My left boot kicks hard through the ball, and the goal umpire doesn't move as the Sherrin (or balloon, when forced to play in the hallway) sails over his head to rapturous applause and adulation from my teammates, my family and all the fans. Fists are pumped, hugs are shared and I'm chaired off the ground in celebration. I think I played that scenario out hundreds of times.

And then, in under-10s, playing for the mighty Glen Iris Gladiators, it happened. It wasn't a Grand Final, but other than that minor detail, the rest was a carbon copy of what I had imagined. I loved footy with all my heart, but it wasn't enough just to love it, to play with my mates and enjoy it – I wanted to make a mark in a heroic moment. I wanted the pressure, the front-and-centre focus, the adulation and the external validation.

This moment is defining for me because it's the first time I can recall the origin of two things: one, the power of my mind to manifest the things I dream into existence and two, the beginning of a turbulent inner battle I would live with for the following decades. It was a battle between my authentic self – a place of love, passion, truth and purpose – and my ego, that not-so-little voice inside me crying out to be recognised, to be noticed, to be the centre of attention and to be loved.

I had what I felt was a 'traditional' upper-middle-class liberal Jewish upbringing. My parents were the children of Holocaust survivors who came to Australia in the '50s with a couple of suitcases and a heavy serving of ancestral trauma. Academic and hardworking, they forged wonderful careers for themselves – my father as a GP and professor of medicine, my mother working as an economist and later in human resource management and consulting. Their successes have been extraordinary: PhDs and Orders of Australia just a bite-size serving of the buffet of their achievements. Although they were often working, my folks were loving, caring and affectionate, always there for my sister and me with a compassionate ear and emotional support. Their hard work also enabled my sister and me to enjoy the privilege of diverse extracurricular activities – piano lessons, guitar lessons, art classes, tennis coaching and singing and dance lessons all came courtesy of Mum and Dad. I've realised more and more over the years just how much they sacrificed to give my sister and me every opportunity to succeed.

My sister, Lara, is very different to me. As young kids, I was outgoing, confident and affectionate and had no trouble chatting to anyone and making new friends. I remember being a 3-year-old in Port Douglas, running around the pool to pinch my dad's friend Kevin on the bum. I gave that bum a good old squeeze. Turns out it wasn't Kevin at all ... I don't even think Kevin was on holidays with us, but the random bloke with the red mark on his tush seemed to see the funny side of it all. Lara was considerably shyer and, of course, these personality differences affected our relationship. Sure, we loved each other but, like many siblings, we had our challenging moments as kids. Spats of jealousy turned fierce and occasionally violent. At times it was as petty (yet equally vindictive) as squashing a bunch of grapes in my bed. Classy, right!? Don't get me wrong, it wasn't all one-way traffic. Emotional regulation wasn't my forte, and Lara got the brunt of that ... my folks got the rest.

Apart from those moments, we had beautiful times together, watching *Rage* every Saturday morning, then learning lyrics to our (her) favourite Top 40 songs. I still know all the words to 'Shoop' by Salt-N-Pepa because of her. My favourite movie growing up was the original *Hairspray* film by John Waters because it was her favourite. I thought she was the coolest. I looked up to her, and she became my guide and confidante. Our friendship grew as we progressed into adolescence. We would cook together and watch *Neighbours* and *Home and Away* together. I learned kindness and respect for women from her. I even smoked my first joints with her out of her bedroom window. She is and always will be one of the greatest women I know, and one of my best mates.

As a family, we had regular holidays down the Great Ocean Road. We were also lucky enough to travel to London a couple of times to attend our cousins' bar and bat mitzvahs and almost annually travelled to Queensland during school holidays for Dad's many work conferences. Yep, even on holidays, Dad was still working. There were times when Lara and I wished Mum and Dad were more like other parents. We would complain that Mum never helped out at the school canteen or that neither of them picked us up from school – we hated having to go to after-school care each day. But that's how it was ... my parents valued their successful careers, and they valued providing for us in the ways that their parents couldn't. A private high-school education was high on that list, and they wanted to ensure that was our reality. They wanted us to be somebodies, and they worked hard to give us everything they could to get us there.

Those values seeped deep into my subconscious from a very young age. Although I vowed never to be a workaholic like my folks, some seeds were planted too early, and some roots were too strong to break.

This has been a blessing and a curse for me. It has helped me put my blood, sweat and tears into everything I do, and that's not just figurative. It has taught me to never stop improving, that there's an extra one per cent to find, that I can always work harder, focus harder, always be better. But, at times, it has also riddled me with stress and anxiety, and it has burnt me out on more than one occasion. It created a perfectionist complex around my voice, my body and my appearance and a scarcity mindset around my finances. It has made me behave in ways that are controlling, manipulative, narcissistic, shameful and regrettable. It has made me feel that I, as a human being, am simply not enough unless I'm climbing higher, doing more, achieving more, winning more, becoming more known ... becoming more of a somebody.

The true 'I am'

So, who is Josh Piterman? I'm a spiritual being having a human experience. In Sanskrit, the word is *aham* or 'I am'. I am the awareness – the soul that is formless, spaceless and timeless. A fragment of the collective consciousness that witnesses all of life's comings and goings and manifests itself as love in its truest and highest form. For some, that would suffice. I also know that, for many of you, at this stage of the book and your journey, that possibly sounds like smacked-out woo-woo crazy talk. Don't worry, you'll be up to speed by the end of Chapter 3.

I can also approach who I am on a human level, and from a personality perspective, which I believe is just as important. What are my core values? Well, I'm a passionate, disciplined, loving, cheeky, curious, playful and adventurous person who is hardwired for connection, communication and storytelling. Working this out has been one of the greatest tools for finding deeper meaning and greater bliss in my life. Sure, there are many times when I don't feel or lean into these things, when I fall into the trap of the ego, back into my anxieties, insecurities and neuroses, but then I find my way back to my truth, then back to the ego and back to truth again. It's a constant dance with a lifetime of choreography to play out – hopefully I can help you learn a few steps.

Like you, I am a human being made perfectly and, at the same time, full of infinite imperfections, which range from my slightly bung toes, to warts I've had on my fingers since I was five, to love handles that thrive off the slightest whiff of anything resembling sugar. I often can't be stuffed putting the bins out and squash everything down for days until I'm met with the impending doom of walking to my outside bins with a stinky trail of bin juice. I promise you I clean that up, with a double dose of disinfectant and equal amounts of shame. I do this often, and my lazy arse never seems to learn! And, at times, I can be overly emotional, defensive, righteous, hypersensitive, insecure and needy. This is all a part of the human predicament, one that we all face on the journey to deeper awareness. We need to have great compassion for ourselves and the parts of us that remain imperfect – they're often covering up our more wounded parts.

Hosting episodes of the *Behind The Mask* podcast, it's clear from listening to a broad spectrum of guests that imperfections are what connect us. We can aspire to others' success and seemingly perfect lifestyles but, where perfectionism separates us, imperfections connect us. When we celebrate our imperfections, enjoy them with a smile, self-deprecate about them, cry about them or simply lean into them, we offer a safe space for others to do the same. (The irony that I had to put on a mask to begin seeing the 'nobody' behind the mask is not lost on me.)

Whether you're in a flow or not, take a moment now to stop reading. This is possibly the first time an author has ever asked you to do that, but I promise to remain consistent on that front.

Journal exercise: who are you?

If you were to put your career to one side, or separate yourself from the roles and identities that you feel define you, who are you? What are your core values and beliefs? What do you stand for? What are the unconditional qualities that do define you? WRITE. THEM. DOWN! You'll be needing them. Keep adding to them as you work through the book as well.

Now, ask yourself: Do I feel enough? Because you *are* enough, those unconditional qualities that make you authentically you will always be enough, even if at times you might not think you are.

You can write that down too!

Marketing the 'not-enoughness' epidemic

'Somebody training' is just another way of saying that the world values the human doing over the human being. That's not to say that we shouldn't value what we do or what someone else does. If anything, it's the opposite: we should have immense respect and reverence for what we do. This is about acknowledging that, first and foremost, we are human beings, and we should work just as hard, if not harder, on that.

One example of this is the Australian education system. Sadly, it still values a certain type of intelligence over another. Academia is considered more valuable than other pursuits, namely creative ones. I think it's a joke to mark one subject up for being 'difficult' and another down for being 'easy'. In the way that a drama student who has a gift for communication, storytelling and language may find it challenging to uncover the intricacies of an advanced maths or physics equation, I can almost assure you that the same would happen if the situation was reversed and someone whose genius lies in figures and numbers had to present a Shakespearean monologue. There is a well-known quote, 'Everybody is a genius, but if you judge a fish by its ability to climb a tree, it will spend its whole life believing it is stupid.' There's something in that for everyone.

What a difference it would make to people and their self-esteem if society supported their unique gifts, rather than what it considered valuable. Imagine if, instead of defaulting to scores and numbers to say how good or bad we are at something, we focused instead on the pursuit of greatness or mastery, regardless of what it's in? This isn't to say there's anything wrong with being great at maths or science – we need doctors, scientists and accountants. The problem is that by valuing some expertise more than other types, it causes so much upset and so many feelings of unworthiness for young creatives. We all have innate talents, and it would be nice if society, social and institutional, could help everyone realise their full potential in those talents. All the current system does is tell us that what we're interested in is probably rubbish, and we could always be better at something else.

Unfortunately, this is just one of the consequences of a society that values the human doing over the human being. Another is a very serious 'not-enoughness' epidemic. Some of this is based on our past traumas, and some is a result of deep-rooted societal constructs (like the ones we just talked about). We are born into a society of implied inadequacy, one that is constantly telling us that we need more – more of this or more of that. Most marketing (and it's literally everywhere) preys on our inbuilt fear around self-worth, constantly strengthening the intrinsic idea that we, as human beings, are simply not enough until we have more money, more followers, a new pair of jeans, a new TV, a new car, new job, new face, new bum. But these are all external – things outside of our true selves that we have been led to believe will make us happy if we acquire or consume them, that having them will mean we are enough. But while these things might offer a brief moment of pleasure or happiness, it doesn't last long. As a society, we're doing laps on the scarcity train, constantly looking for something new.

Now, there's nothing wrong with wanting external stuff. We all need money to live, clothes to put on our back and a roof over our heads, so I'm not saying we should forego all extrinsic desires. The problem occurs when those extrinsic desires are deemed more valuable than our intrinsic ones and govern our self-worth.

Social media has only added to this by constantly pitting us against the curated highlights of another person's life and using algorithms that feed us what they think we want more of. It's just more unhealthy comparison, and a vicious cycle, one that billions of people, me included, get caught in. Argh! Get me out of here!

What I've learned is that the only way to get off the not-enoughness train is by becoming conscious of it. When we do that, we create a buffer between our true selves and our egos and begin addressing life and all the marketing in it with awareness and discernment. Do I need that new bum, or do I want it? If so, why do I want it? What's wrong with my current bum? Has Kim Kardashian been circulating through my Instagram feed a lot lately, which is now giving me an inferiority complex about the state of my existing bum? Am I going to be a better human being for changing my bum? Could I just go to the gym and do some squats, which would have an array of other positive benefits? These are all important questions to ask to be discerning and responsible in our choices, rather than simply reacting to the next big craze, suppressing our feelings about ourselves and seeking immediate validation instead.

All this aside, regardless of the systems we exist in and the countless challenges to our self-worth, it would be a cop-out to blame our not-enoughness epidemic purely on things out of our control. We can all choose what we buy into. We must become hypervigilant, emotionally responsible and aware of this in order to remain inwardly contented in the modern world. We all have parts of ourselves we feel are ugly, shameful or painful – things that we are scared to look at or share because we fear they will make us unworthy or unlovable. But, once we are honest with ourselves and begin to understand that our imperfections, insecurities and inadequacies actually make us more worthy, loved, seen and connected to others (and to ourselves), we begin to take off our rusted masks and feel that we, as human beings, are enough.

But we can't just click our fingers and change all of this –

it's a process. So, how do we shift from mask on to mask off?

First, we have to have the courage to be vulnerable.

Starting your nobody training

Have you ever reached a goal thinking it'll change who you are in some way, but it doesn't? It can be a confronting feeling. When it happened to me, I had this overwhelming feeling that I had been deceived. I had made it to the peak of my career, but I was still a prisoner to one of society's great systemic problems. I had been taught to appreciate people's successes and achievements more than their innate qualities, values and characteristics. Even more sadly, I had scored myself under the same system.

When I realised I had hit the top but I still felt so empty, I knew something wasn't right. There had to be more to life than work, goals, achievements and titles, right?

During my time playing the Phantom in London in 2019, and subsequently into the early stages of the Covid pandemic, I began to recognise a space between who I am as a person and what I do for a career. You could say that 'nobody training' was subconsciously starting to creep in. I suppose that when you've been playing a role like the Phantom, on London's West End, something that very few Australians have ever done, you could be forgiven for allowing your ego to convince you that you're defined by what you do. Once again, the bloke quite literally wears a mask, but I suppose that achieving such a major milestone and not feeling different as a person at all only justified my new-found theory of 'identity separation'. To me, this was the separation of the human doing from the human being.

Somewhat ironically, the Phantom's relationship with his mask is quite literally a metaphor for his relationship with his ego. Aside from being a creative genius, he has a deformity, which he resents and is ashamed of. But, when he puts on that iconic half-face mask to hide the deformity, he believes he can be the version of himself that will be loved, admired and respected. When he isn't wearing it, the true self comes out: a dark, frightened, vulnerable and insecure man child, who has no capacity to truly love someone else because he doesn't know how to love himself. Art always has a funny way of holding a mirror up to us, making us see ourselves in a new way.

While I was leaning into the theory of 'identity separation', contemplating it often in the stopping that came with Covid, I came across renowned mindset coach Ben Crowe on social media. Ben had predominantly spent his time working with elite athletes, like tennis players Andre Agassi and Ash Barty, Formula 1 driver Daniel Ricciardo, cricketer Alex Carey, a host of Olympic athletes and some of the Richmond Football Club (AFL). He now works with organisations like the UN and the World Health Organization. I was taken by his philosophies and teachings, and his knack for finding simple, functional solutions to highly complex internal issues.

Ben validated so much of what I had been ruminating on at a time when I needed it most. I have always prided myself on being a 'glass-half-full' person, so Ben's approach for flipping things on their head to see life through an alternate lens to find a positive outcome really spoke to me. I think there is always an opportunity to find healthy positives in shitty situations. But as Jelena Dokic says in season one of the *Behind The Mask* podcast, 'It's a fine line between a positive mindset and toxic positivity.' I firmly agree with this – it's very easy in shitty situations to pretend like everything is okay when it clearly isn't. But suppression is never the answer, and it never ends well. So, as a performer who could no longer do or share what I loved most, I had to acknowledge how shit this was but also see how there could be positives. It became an incredible opportunity for study and self-reflection. If you can't go outside, go inside.

We are all going to be faced with suffering in our lives. That is an inevitability of the human condition. Nobody is immune to suffering. Sometimes, these things are out of our control, like a pandemic. So, it's not whether or not these things happen that truly matters, but rather how we respond to them. In fact, I would argue that there is no better teacher in life than suffering, if you choose to learn from it and through it.

My intention for the Covid sabbatical was to use that suffering as an opportunity to begin nobody training. Not necessarily to fix everything and become perfect or reach enlightenment, but to work through some of these layers of conditioning, trauma and addiction. However, if you're going to do this kind of work, you need to be prepared for the fact that it's not easy. It's muddy, sticky and crunchy. More like 'endarkenment'. You have to relinquish control and be prepared to get dirty. It can bring up a hell of a lot of painful stuff, and it did for me.

As humans, we either face this sort of trauma head-on or watch as it negatively impacts our lives. It certainly negatively impacted my internal world, even if the people who saw me thought I was killing it! We have a duty as humans to address our shit. So, I had some tough questions to ask myself, the sort of questions most of us steer clear of. What parts of myself hadn't I looked at? What was I avoiding? What flaws in my character needed addressing? What were my addictions? What other traumas had I not dealt with? Where was there scope for improvement, and how could that improvement benefit not just me, but all my relationships? These are the sorts of questions that, if you're willing to be vulnerable and truly sit in them, will crack you open. After asking myself some hard questions, it was clear to me that I couldn't do this all alone. I needed guidance – I needed a mentor.

Often what we are seeking is also seeking us, and my relationship with Ben didn't end on Instagram. I was introduced to him via our mutual friend Michael Cassel, a wonderful man and great theatrical producer who has always unconditionally believed in me as a person. I spent a day with Ben in Melbourne in early 2021, which led to many more exchanges over the subsequent years. He has changed my life. Ben always has a nugget of wisdom to share, including in season two of the *Behind The Mask* podcast, and he's one of the most influential role models in my life. I owe so many elements of this book to the guidance I received from him and the journey it's taken me on.

Learning to be vulnerable

The opposite of wearing a mask is to be metaphorically naked. It's to show up as our true selves, with all our wounds and scars, and still have the courage to say, 'I'm here, I have nothing to hide, and I embrace this world openly and authentically.' This is vulnerability.

Throughout the many episodes of the *Behind The Mask* podcast, I've been constantly blown away by the bravery of the guests who have the courage to face their deepest discomforts and demons head-on. These people may not all have run ultramarathons like Grace Tame, or won sixteen doubles Grand Slams like Todd Woodbridge (both have appeared on the show), but they're prepared to live life with a growth mindset, embracing the thoughts and emotions that constantly fly through them rather than suppressing them or running away from them. They truly acknowledge their flaws, shame and traumas. They own their shit. They are living proof of the immense power and freedom that comes from being vulnerable enough to say, 'Hey, I'm not okay. I'm messy. I'm struggling. I'm scared. I fucked up. But I'm here, unmasked, owning it all and still trying to be the best version of myself.'

There are many ways we can become brave enough to willingly take off our masks. Seeing a therapist is a common Western choice, one that I've done and still do regularly. I've also found a lot of self-healing in various forms of yoga. Sitting uncomfortable in a fairly inflexible body and allowing pain to arise without judging it or myself (often failing dismally) has been incredible for leaning into my internal self and learning about my mental and emotional discomfort. Shakira once said, 'My hips don't lie' – she obviously spends a lot of time in a strong vinyasa flow, because I know how she feels. For anyone who's done a bit of yoga, you'll know that our hips store a hell of a lot of emotion. Cut to me being the dude in the corner of the class crying through another lengthy half pigeon pose. But I've learned that many life lessons can be found on a yoga mat, far more than I anticipated. It has been a powerful way to learn to be present and not run away from the feelings (physical and emotional) that come up during class.

I've also meditated consistently for over a decade; stepped into innumeral ice baths; done plenty of breath work (pranayama); seen energetic healers, mindset coaches, hypnotherapists and Chinese medicine practitioners; participated in countless spiritual workshops; taken my fair share of plant medicine; and I love an ecstatic dance party (google that one and get along, they're wild!). Sometimes I've walked out of experiences with my heart open and my mind blown, and sometimes I have spent hours of my life with nothing to show, but all of these experiences have been an incredible doorway to facilitating my philosophical, spiritual and self-healing journey. There is no good or bad when it comes to self-inquiry, it simply is, so I acknowledge them all with deep reverence for the wisdom and lessons they've taught me. However, ultimately they are just a vehicle, a gateway – it's always me who is responsible for doing the work. The same goes for you on your journey. You can read this book many times over but it's just another tool filled with tools. It's up to you to pick them up and use them.

A conscious descent

One of the most profound therapeutic experiences I have ever taken part in, which required a hell of a lot of vulnerability, was attending a men's circle during the start of Covid in 2020. It was a fairly challenging moment in my life, having just found out that the original production of *The Phantom of the Opera* on the West End was now closing down, and I was officially out of a job. I had shared a dinner table and sung for King Charles only a few days before lockdown at what was his last major social engagement (I think he may have given me Covid, or I gave it to him ... shh, don't tell anyone), and suddenly it felt like someone had pushed me off the edge of a cliff. I was caught between experiencing the heights of the life I had dreamed of and landing face-first in a painful reality. I had worked so hard for this opportunity, and the realisation it was all over was incredibly difficult. One of the few philosophical consolations was that it was due to something entirely out of my control, and there were bigger concerns at the time than my unemployment. Although this made the pill easier to swallow, it didn't stop the feeling of freefalling.

I recall a long conversation on the phone with my good friend and mentor Asher Packman (who appears alongside Ben Crowe in season two of the *Behind The Mask* podcast), while traipsing through Clapham Common in London's southwest on one of those 'get me the fuck out of the house, I'm convinced I'm going batshit crazy' lockdown strolls. Asher is a wise owl, one of those men who has lived a thousand lives. He has ridden the emotional waves of cancer and experienced loss in profound and tragic ways. Asher's wisdom knows no bounds. He helped me realise there could be some wonderful lessons during the pandemic. He says that if we are to freefall off a metaphorical cliff, it's an opportunity to 'descend consciously'.

We can only meet things as deeply as we've met ourselves so, in order to fully understand what the universe is throwing at us, Asher suggests, 'We need to grab a broom and a torch, go into the cellar of our souls, shine a light into its corners and see what needs dusting out.'

I decided to sign up to his 'The Way' course. This was incredible medicine for me during 2020: Zoom sessions where twenty-plus men from around the globe took off their masks and shared openly with bravery and vulnerability. We studied the great Swiss psychiatrist Carl Jung, as well as famous mytho-poet Robert Bly and American writer

Joseph Campbell. We learned about Jungian archetypes and our shadows and gifts, meditated on death, analysed the wounds we receive from our mothers and fathers and explored the wisdom, truth and beauty of ancient myth and poetry. Through our shared pain and struggles, we found healing individually and collectively.

Many of us dusted out those cobwebs, explored our 'endarkenment' and shone a light on some very deep wounds that required the most tender love, care and understanding. We found hidden gems in those wounds, and many men from the course still take part in a monthly circle that I attend regularly in Melbourne. After all, as the brilliant Canadian breath coach Steve Beattie says, 'The lone wolf is in his head, the wolfpack are in their hearts.'

We all have a *heart* story to tell about our life's journey, and the great mythological stories of the world help us make sense of ours. When we hear and share those stories authentically from a truly open and vulnerable place, they transcend the individual and become universal. Our connection to each other is innate. It's old wisdoms like these circles that enable a unique space for healing.

Have you ever been part of a group circle? How could you benefit from shared healing experiences? I believe in the power of circle for all genders so, if that speaks to you, I recommend it. There are countless circles out there for all genders – google as a starting point and see what calls to you. If you are practising yoga, breath work or Pilates; have a gym community; or attend any sort of religious establishment, then this is also a great place to ask around.

For men, I think Asher's 'The Fifth Direction', which is online, is absolutely brilliant and I highly recommend it.

If nothing else, hearing other people talk about their lives and struggles reminds you that you're not alone. There are more people who feel the same as you than you think.

Journal exercise: heart stories

What is your 'heart story'? How can you go about finding ways to embrace it and share it bravely, openly and vulnerably? I recommend writing out your heart story – something in your life that you would usually hide away – something you carry shame about or feel less worthy because of. Write it out, get it out of your body and on paper. It can be very healing.

A rising tide lifts all boats

Once you start on your journey of self-discovery in earnest, you will get insight into how things might be for other people as well. This can be a heavy experience if it's not something you've spent a lot of time thinking about! It will likely reveal parts of yourself that you struggle to be compassionate towards and therefore the parts of others that you equally lack compassion for. Once again, we meet things (and people) at the level we've met ourselves.

The other way we show a lack of enoughness is in the way we talk about and behave towards others. It's Mum's old saying, 'If you don't have anything nice to say, don't say anything at all'. Turns out the mums of the world aren't just there to be a constant reference point for all our triggers and traumas – they can also embody love in the highest form.

Of course, we all need to have a vent from time to time, and I don't think there's anything wrong with that as long as we're approaching it consciously, but it's also up to us to check ourselves. That might mean asking ourselves: When did we last sit with a friend and compliment them? When did we last talk about a friend positively rather than having a good old bitch about them? And did we bitch about them because of something they did, or because we felt threatened by them and needed to dim their light to make ours shine brighter?

A rising tide lifts all boats. We feel so much better talking well of people we love (and even the ones we don't feel we love) than talking ill of them. We would also do well to ask ourselves: What is there to be gained from talking about other people poorly? Could my emotional energy be better spent elsewhere?

You will also start asking yourself what judgements or assumptions you are making about situations or someone else's behaviour. We tend to make a lot of assumptions and, on reflection, many weren't worth making. One of the great lessons I learned from Ben Crowe is choosing to make generous assumptions. Most of our assumptions are judgemental and negative. An example of a generous assumption is when someone cuts you off in traffic: rather than hurling abuse at them or complaining about them, assume they're rushing home because they left the oven on, or their child has just been taken to hospital and they're anxiously trying to get there. Generous assumptions are a great way to free yourself of many of life's unnecessary judgements. Ben suggests that we 'judge ourselves on our intentions, but judge others on their behaviour', so by leading with a generous assumption, we can start to feel into another's intention, and this is a great doorway into an expansion of compassion and empathy.

Also, instead of complaining behind their back, if you have an issue with someone's behaviour that needs addressing, approach them calmly and address it, even if it's uncomfortable. Challenging conversations and confrontation are necessary in life, and we all need boundaries when our values and core beliefs are being challenged. We also need to learn how to disagree healthily (see the BTM interview with politicians Zoe McKenzie and Josh Burns for more on this). But treating people like shit behind their back (or to their face, for that matter) simply because we're feeling threatened by them will never help us grow or truly make us feel worthy, loved, valued or enough. It's also terrible karma and a waste of energy.

As I've journeyed through my life in showbiz, people have tried to dim my light. I get it – I'm a big personality. I can take up a lot of space, and I've been self-centred at times, especially in my twenties and early thirties. It's interesting now to reflect that these were probably when my self-esteem was at its lowest. I think that's pretty common – the smaller we feel on the inside, the thicker the masks we wear to compensate. Fortunately, as I've grown older and hopefully somewhat wiser, I've been able to reflect on these situations and see them for what they were.

Dimming the light

Early in my career, I worked as a singer at Tokyo Disney and as a member of The Ten Tenors. There were many tiny acts of bullying, belittling and manipulation by my colleagues, some of whom I believed were my friends.

They included stripping solo singing lines away from me because they didn't want me front and centre, legal threats to deny me incredible opportunities, giving me a translation of soul-crushing notes from a non-English speaking director, only to find out that they weren't the notes at all, and my co-star completely ignoring me for days, knowing full well the anxiety this would provoke. Some people have apologised, and others I've never seen again.

I don't hate anyone for treating me poorly. It's just a reflection of their suffering and where they're at on their growth and healing journey. Those who are full of light don't need to dim anyone else's but, as a young artist, these things were terribly confusing and painful and made me feel even more inadequate, insecure and unworthy.

Part of what helped me was my clear vision and my unwavering desire to live out my dreams. That gave me a focus and a confidence that kept me moving forward even if I was deeply hurt at times. For a lot of people, however, this sort of behaviour can really affect them to the point where they leave their workplaces or even their professions. That's a sad and painful reality.

If you sit with yourself and acknowledge that you behave in this way, rather than projecting outwards, spend time going inwards. Ask yourself why you feel *your* light isn't shining brightly enough. What are *you* not receiving from someone else that you can give yourself? You might find it beneficial to have some raw, open discussions with the people you love most, or to seek the help of a psychologist, counsellor or some other form of therapist or healing modality.

You may face moments like this in your work or personal life. My advice based on many years of dealing with this is to call it out. Call out the bullying, the belittling, the sly little digs and the vile actions. The more we stay silent, the more we enable. I've done plenty of enabling in my time, and every time I've allowed it, I'm the only one who ends up suffering. It's happened in relationships, with cast members, with directors and even with producers. Once upon a time, I was taught to ignore that bullying, that it's water off a duck's back. Well, very often it's not. It festers inside you and makes you feel like shit, so confront it. Whether you talk to the individual directly or intervene through a third party, be grounded and clear about what you need to change. That way, if it doesn't change, you can walk away proudly knowing that you were true to who you are and what you stand for. And, who knows ... maybe that person will eventually mature and finally be able to take on your feedback.

The wound and the gift

Carl Jung once said, 'The genius hides behind the wound.' Each person has a set of gifts, skills and talents that is their unique genius – our special thing that we offer to the world. On the flipside, we are also all wounded. And, like night and day, the world has a way of finding equilibrium. As we discover, embrace and expand the wonder of our gifts, so too do we continue to identify, explore and hopefully heal our wounds. Sadly, for some the wound grows until it is too painful to bear. In showbiz, we see this with fame and stardom all the time, particularly those whose light burns brightest. A lot of light can make for some very large wounds and, when I think of great artists like Amy Winehouse, Kurt Cobain or Heath Ledger, to name just a few, I can't help but feel a deep sense of sadness.

If you had told me when I was fifteen that by my late thirties I would have played the Phantom and Jean Valjean, two of the most iconic roles in musical theatre, on the West End, I probably would've laughed in your face. Firstly, because a career as a singer and actor wasn't even on the radar, and secondly because I couldn't tell you the first thing about musicals, let alone those two.

It wasn't like playing music was totally off the radar.

I had learned piano as a kid (absolutely hated it, equally regret not continuing it), guitar for a few years from year 7 and was even in a cover band in year 9 whose name I can't even remember. I did, however, love telling stories. I loved chatting with anyone, no matter their age or gender. My mates loved getting me to break the ice with girls they had never met while they watched on awkwardly from afar. I loved the chats and equally got off on returning to my mates with stories after the inevitable, 'So ... what'd they say?' The same mates were also constantly weirded out by the conversations I would have with their parents at their houses, but I legitimately enjoyed it. I loved sharing stories and thoughts about school, sport and politics and, of course, regularly throwing their sons under the bus.

My first real venture into musicals happened because, as 16-year-olds, my friends and I became obsessed with Michael Jackson. And yes, I'm aware that sentence doesn't read so well these days. The MJ anniversary concert was on TV, and it was all the rage. I was blown away by his songs, his craftsmanship, his stage presence, his star power and, of course, his dance moves. I *had* to learn how to moonwalk. I must have killed the VHS recording rewinding and fast forwarding as much as I did to break the movements down. But, after working out what he was actually doing with weight transfer, I began practising until I nailed it.

I don't know what possessed me ... you might just call it fate (and an incessant desire for show-ponying), but one day

I decided that moonwalking in the senior college cafeteria was what the moment required. Little did I know that the director of the school musical, Mr Hann (Dawson) was watching on. So, I'm midway through reversing this bad-arse move, feeling pretty great about myself, when I get a tap on the shoulder from Dawson. I turn around quickly, glowing with slight embarrassment. 'Have you ever done a musical?' he asked. 'No, Mr Hann,' I respond, fearing that mentioning my year 7 experience as the security guard in *Germs: The Musical* would not help me get whatever may eventuate from this encounter. He said, 'We're doing a production of *Fame* the musical this year, and we could use some dance moves like that onstage. Would you be interested in auditioning?' I said, 'Sure, why not?'

I spent the couple of weeks before the audition being scared of what people would think of me (this is pre-*Glee*, remember, cool straight boys didn't perform), and listening to the cast recording/watching the original movie version from the '80s. Side note: that film is absolutely iconic and, in my humble opinion, shits on the musical. No offence to anyone involved in the creation of that stage show, but that script must've been written in a fromagerie. Thankfully, as a year 11 novice who knew close to nothing about musicals, I loved it, so I put any fears around the shit I was about to cop aside and rocked up to the audition.

There was plenty of nervous energy as I walked into the group audition room. Somewhere along the line, Dawson pulls me aside and says he's interested in having me audition for the role of Tyrone Jackson, a young black dancer from a low socioeconomic upbringing. Of course, these days that just wouldn't fly, but in 2002 at a private school with next to no young black men, nobody even questioned it. I'm glad we've evolved well beyond this in the past twenty-odd years. My Tyrone Jackson audition required some singing, dancing and rapping. I was a pretty big rap fan in those days. I had bought plenty of '90s and '00s hip-hop albums – Eminem, Dre, Jurassic 5 and Wu-Tang – so I was pretty comfortable with that genre, although on reflection I'm sure it was all incredibly lame and culturally inappropriate. The dance part was just an opportunity to show off a few more MJ moves I would be finessing (the side moonwalk was well and truly in my arsenal now) as well as learning some breakdancing and some ballet, which I actually thought was pretty bloody cool. The singing was the scary part. I had never done much before, especially at this level, and it freaked me out. But I embraced it all and got through it with blind confidence, immeasurable amounts of passion and a big, fat boyish charm mask on.

I was asked to play the role and immediately entered the amazing, crazy, intense and extraordinary world of high-school musicals. Wow! I had never come across anything like this. I couldn't believe what I was experiencing or what I had been missing out on. I had only ever felt camaraderie of any kind on the sporting field, and this was like that on steroids.

Add to that the opportunity of performing live onstage, the immediate positive adulation and the reality of socialising with girls much more, and it was probably more of a steroid for the ego. Unbeknownst to my unaware 16-year-old self, this beautiful gift of performing and communicating was also playing right into my oldest wounds – my desire to be front and centre, to be acknowledged, seen, known, valued, validated, applauded and loved. Jung was absolutely bang on!

The rejection gateway

We wear our masks to protect us against myriad things. Sometimes we wear them to avoid the hurt in the first place, and other times we wear them because we have been hurt and we don't want to feel that way again.

When it comes to wounds, we can all empathise with the feeling of rejection, particularly the stories our egos create around it and how they can affect our self-worth. When I teach, mentor and facilitate BTM workshops with students and recent musical theatre graduates stepping into the showbiz industry, they often ask me how I deal with all the 'no's that come with auditioning. How do I not take it personally?

Now, I'm not an expert on many things, but as a performer I consider myself an absolute pro at being rejected. Over ninety per cent of my career has been rejection – it's like speed dating through song ... generally it doesn't go so well. People often say, 'You've got to have a thick skin to do what you do.' I think that's a cop-out, because it suggests that the only way to deal with rejection is with a stiff upper lip and a whole bunch of repressed and suppressed feelings, or some more masks! Sounds really healthy, right?

Through reflection over the years, I have broken rejection down into four key ideas that really helped me rethink it and its place in my life and career.

First, I like to think of it as having agency – I have choices. Note that this applies to all job interviews, presentations, performances and, of course, hot dates. Firstly, and most importantly, I have agency. I'm not kidnapped at gunpoint and dragged into the audition room. I decide to put myself out there for the role. I am also very conscious of what I get to choose and what the panel gets to choose. I make sure that I'm prepared for the audition and that I've given it the consideration and time it deserves. I get to choose what song or songs I sing; they get to choose what they want to hear. I get to choose how I want to share the material on the page and how I interpret the character – that's my job as an artist. They get to choose if they would like to see more and, if so, how they would like to direct me. I get to choose how I interpret that direction. They get to choose whether I progress to the next round, whether I'm the right look, ethnicity, height and all that and whether I get the job. I get to choose how I respond to that information.

The second part is the most important part when it comes to rejection: self-worth. The panel never, ever gets to choose my self-worth. It's up to me whether I've done a good job or not, and that isn't contingent on me getting the role. Whether I get it or not, I make sure I can look back objectively and ask myself whether I shared work that I'm proud of. If the answer is yes, then that's all there is to it. If there are improvements to be made, then I can work hard to improve for next time. Once we learn to embody these first two ideas, agency and self-worth, we shift past the dints to our ego and the idea that rejection is a reflection on us as a person.

The third part is about non-attachment. When we go into an audition with a strong focus on choice and self-worth, we are far less likely to be fixated on an outcome. We know our place in the audition room, so we come to auditions with the desire to freely share, rather than needing something in return or being defined by the results. We see it as an opportunity, not a need, and therefore we tend to focus on the process rather than the result. And that's the place where all the magic happens!

The final part is where philosophy takes over. What I've really learned in my time as a performer is that all rejection is doing is leading us towards a situation where we *are* accepted. Rejection in and of itself is a gateway to acceptance. We just have to learn to trust it. Of course, I'm not going to say that rejection isn't utterly heartbreaking at first but, once we've sat with that pain, we would do well to take Rumi's words on board, 'You have to keep breaking your heart until it opens.' This quote has served me well over the years, professionally and personally.

The screaming soprano

In late 2018, right at the end of my run of *Beautiful: The Carole King Musical*, I auditioned for a supporting role in the Disney musical version of *Aladdin*. After just having spent a year doing eight shows a week, I wasn't excited about doing that again immediately, but I thought it might be fun and it was an opportunity for more paid work. I didn't mind what the outcome was, I was completely non-attached, and this was a powerful blessing. The role wasn't something I would normally throw my hat in the ring for, it was comedic and slapsticky, but all of that meant complete freedom.

I progressed all the way to the final round. I sang and acted well, but I didn't completely nail the dance call (always my weak spot) even though I did my best. With no pressure or expectation on my shoulders, I really enjoyed the process and had a great time exploring the role. Creating a light-hearted funny character was totally joyous, and a far cry from the darkness of my character in *Beautiful*. The audition experience was excellent.

A couple of weeks later, I had finished *Beautiful* and was holidaying in Byron Bay, walking along the magical Wategos Beach. For those who haven't been, it's one of the most magnificent beaches in Australia, where the clear water blends seamlessly into shades of greens and blue, calling you to dive in, and the whales, dolphins and turtles regularly stop by to say 'G'day' while they share a morning dip with the local swimmers and surfers.

I was enjoying the view when my phone rang; it was my

manager, James. He had that slightly spritely tone, the one I've learned is there to cheer me up if things don't quite go my way. After asking how Byron was, he said, 'Mate, look, I heard from Disney. It was between you and another guy in the end and, unfortunately, they've gone with him. I'm really sorry.' I remember standing on a few jagged rocks, looking out across the vast expanse of the most easterly point in Australia, and being completely at ease with that news. 'That's okay,' I said. 'Thanks for the call, I'm sure something else will come up.'

It would have been nice to land it. It was an 18-month contract and, as a performer, that's great financial security. I had just bought my first home and could've used a little cash to lower the mortgage but, in that moment, I didn't feel any sense of scarcity or disappointment. Maybe I wasn't overly excited about the role, maybe I was due a holiday after *Beautiful* or maybe subconsciously I knew that rejection is the gateway to acceptance. Either way, it was fine.

Ten months later, I'm sitting in the bistro of one of those very prestigious ties-and-jackets, members only clubs in Sydney, when I get a call from a UK number. It's my former agent, Lauren, calling from London. I answer it as inconspicuously as possible. 'Hello,' I whisper. 'Hi Josh, hope you're great. Hey, would you like to play the Phantom in *The Phantom of the Opera* on the West End? Because the team over here would love you to.' I was right, rejection was my gateway to acceptance! If I had been doing *Aladdin*, I wouldn't have been able to take this opportunity. I immediately felt a rush of inner soprano and I screamed louder and higher than I ever had before and, of course, security promptly and swiftly escorted me out of the bistro!

There's a saying that 'fail' actually stands for first attempt in learning, but I prefer 'forever acknowledging invaluable lessons'. Once we take on those lessons and approach the possibility of rejection with an open heart, fully embracing the possibility of it happening but knowing we are enough and worthy regardless of the outcome, then we are no longer scared. We are no longer fearful of our worth being dependant on a particular outcome, we are no longer desperate – we are just enjoying being ourselves in the moment with no attachments to a particular result. When we apply these theories, we are far more likely to explore the breadth of our creativity, far more present in the work, far more willing to play and take risks and far less likely to take things personally or come across as desperate. What profound lessons! Now we have agency again, and that is freedom.

Shame and blame – an imposter's dance

Another reason that we wear masks is to separate ourselves from the things we have done. For many people, me included, the feeling of shame is too overwhelming to carry. Sometimes, we don't have the capacity to own up to and be responsible for our shameful words and actions. This is where shame dances with blame in a piece of choreography that leaves a trail of destruction. Rather than owning our behaviour, acknowledging our actions and imperfections and pointing the finger within, we point the finger at others and blame them instead, often the actual victim. We've all done it, and we know that it only causes misery and upset for all.

Shame is a natural feeling, but it's not nice to experience. In fact, it's certifiably bloody awful. It sits festering away at the solar plexus, relentlessly reminding us of regrettable or embarrassing behaviour. We have all done things that we hold shame or guilt about. For example, during *Les Misérables*, we'd had a long day performing at West End LIVE followed by a matinee and evening performance. I was tired and wired. At the end of the show, I felt so relieved that, in my ecstatic celebration with another cast member, I kissed them on the lips. They immediately pulled me up on it, and I felt shame straight away, that sinking pain in my chest. What had I done? That was so inappropriate! I apologised profusely. I knew it was wrong the moment it happened, and fortunately we dealt with it straight afterwards, but I felt terrible for them and it took me a while to let the feeling of shame go.

Because these feelings fester, you need to deal with them immediately. When someone calls you out, or when you know you've done something wrong, it's better to own it, apologise for it and responsibly deal with the repercussions as well as you can rather than diverting your shame into blame. Acknowledge that you did it but, instead of beating yourself up about it, ask yourself what you can do to stop it from happening again.

Phantom of the panic attack

On the thirty-fourth anniversary of *The Phantom of the Opera*, I was unwell. I'd had one of the various seasonal London colds you're almost guaranteed to get, served up with a side of mild laryngitis – a deliciously snotty and throaty concoction!

If it had been any other day of the week, I would have rested up and come back to work in a few days fit, fresh and firing. But it was a special day celebrating the show, and I wanted to be a part of it. I wanted to feel important and (ironically, in hindsight) I wanted to be seen as the masked man. So, I decided to give it a crack. And boy, did I give it a crack. Cracks here, cracks there, my voice was cracking everywhere. It was potentially the most cracktastic (maybe even craptastic) version of 'Music of the Night' ever.

At interval, the concerned creatives came into my dressing room for the challenging conversation as to whether I could continue. After it was clear I couldn't, they decided to put the understudy on for Act 2. I was extremely grateful to him for embracing the pressures of the situation so graciously, but I was equally devastated.

I left the theatre crestfallen and cried the whole cab ride home and well into the night. I felt so embarrassed, so ashamed of my performance, of my decision to go on when I clearly couldn't perform. I felt that I had let the show, the team, the fans and myself down. I felt like an imposter, one that was having a fairly severe panic attack.

This is the other form of shame, the shame we carry quietly. It's shame about the parts of ourselves that we deem inadequate. We are afraid that people will see them. Shame disconnects us from the world because it makes us feel like we're unworthy of belonging in it. We believe that, if people see these parts of us, we won't be liked or accepted, or we'll be cut off.

In the previous story, I was afraid of being seen as unable to do my role. As a performer, I've experienced shame like this many times when I don't feel I've nailed that scene, that song or that performance, or when I'm not able to do my job because I'm unwell or physically/vocally exhausted. It comes with guilt and embarrassment that I'm not perfect. It penetrates my solar plexus with a fear that the audience, my fellow actors or the creative team won't like *me* because I've done a version of *my performance* that I don't like. How bizarre is the idea that a subjective review of my *human doing* might be enough for another person to not appreciate my *human being*.

Imposter syndrome

Imposter syndrome is the idea that you are undeserving or unworthy of your position or success, and that you're a fake or a fraud who is going to be found out. Often, imposter syndrome comes from the fear of not living up to our own unrealistic expectations for ourselves. This is something many performers grapple with. 'Shit! They're gonna see that I can't do this, that I'm no good and they should've cast someone else.' That's certainly how I felt after the birthday incident. I remember getting a beautifully empathetic email from the company the following day but, when we are dealing with imposter syndrome, we often fail to hear others who are honestly validating us and giving us positive feedback. This can result in us doubling down and working harder and harder. I've been guilty of this and yes, it often gets results, but generally from a place of fear.

It is clear, therefore, that when experiencing imposter syndrome, our confidence is always lower than our competence. You may have countless people honestly praising you, validating you, acknowledging how competent you are, but if your confidence is low because you haven't reached your own high expectations (which are often above your level of competency) you tend to feel like an imposter.

When it comes to dealing with imposter syndrome, some people believe that you just have to 'fake it till you make it'. But that's another cop-out and only fuels a toxic internal relationship, as many people 'make it' and still feel like a fake. I believe we need to be prepared to acknowledge our imposter syndrome consciously with self-love. When we bring self-compassion to imposter syndrome, we realise we might be winging it (but so is everyone), but we aren't faking it at all, we're simply exploring the distance between where we are and where we want to be. On that journey, perfectionism is impossible and it's normal and natural to make a whole bunch of mistakes. As Asher says in the BTM podcast, 'perfectionism is a death'. Once something is perfect, there's nowhere else for it to go – it ends. The dance of life happens in the imperfection. Therefore, I've learned that the best antidote to imposter syndrome is to lower my expectations of myself (and others), to enjoy the parts of me that are winging it, to embrace my mistakes and celebrate my imperfections as fully and as fearlessly as possible and to dance the dance.

Journal exercise: knowing your inner imposter

What's your relationship like with imposter syndrome? Do you ever feel like a fraud or a fake? Are you a perfectionist? How is this relationship serving you? Could you hold yourself with more self-compassion and self-love and give yourself greater licence to be imperfect? In what ways have mistakes helped you to grow in the past?

Journal on this, then reflect on your answers.

2

PART 2

Fear

Understanding fear

Fear plays a huge part in our lives. We feel it and face it in a variety of forms daily. From a primitive point of view, humans ought to be grateful for fear. It's a wonderful inbuilt thing that helps us survive in the world. We need a certain level of it to stay alive and protect the people we love most. In acknowledging this healthy level of fear, we create ways to alleviate it and keep ourselves safe – seatbelts and airbags in cars, traffic lights and speed limits on roads, children's books for people suffering with hippopotomonstrosesquippedaliophobia (the fear of long words ... oh the irony), just to name a few.

The brain processes fear by sending a message to either the amygdala, when there is a real threat of danger or fear, or the higher cortical centre, when something may be perceived as a threat but doesn't actually 'scare' us. For example, being confronted by a group of threatening men down a dark alley is a response within the amygdala, but the opening night of a musical is probably heading to the cortical centre.

Fortunately, your brain does a lot of this automatically, but that makes it harder for you to untangle a primal response to what may be a very modern problem. For example, seeing a shark fin in the water you're swimming in is a different experience to forgetting a line mid-scene.

Our major primal fears can be grouped as death, failure, abandonment and the unknown. For hundreds of thousands of years, our ancestors have experienced these with life-or-death consequences. Let's explore each of these in a little more detail.

Death: Fear of death can include concerns about pain, injury, illness, crossing the road, the afterlife or the vast array of snakes, spiders and drop bears that will kill you immediately if you ever summon the courage to travel to Australia. Survival is everything for us humans. Fear of death as the ultimate consequence can make living extremely difficult for some people. Think about it: If you're worried about an elevator malfunctioning into a long drop with a short stop, they're going to terrify you. A fear of heights can be debilitating as well. These fears seeping into situations that affect our daily lives can result in anxiety or panic attacks for some people.

Failure: This includes fears around not living up to our potential, not doing things correctly or not being good enough. Fear around our financial situations, nailing that job interview, presentation, audition or opening night are usually fear of failure. It comes from our innate, deep-rooted insecurities that we are not worthy, and being critically judged by others only validates our poor internal belief system. A fear of failure stops us from dreaming big, taking the odd risk and stepping out beyond our comfort zone, the place where our greatest capacity for growth lies.

Abandonment: This includes fears around loneliness, being dumped by your partner or someone not swiping right on your Tinder pic. It also includes feelings of shame, public humiliation or embarrassment, like when your parents were running forty-five minutes late to pick you up from after-school care when you were seven and there you were, sitting on the table, gazing longingly out the window, a single tear sliding down your face in slowmo, counting down the seconds until they arrive. Argh, the trauma's still there ... These are all fears of abandonment, a sense that you will be disconnected from the world or the people in it in some way.

The unknown: Fear around change, the future, other cultures, races or sexual identities, extraterrestrial beings, conspiracy theories and so on are all fear of the unknown. Generally, fear of the unknown comes from an innate human desire to want to control things. This might manifest as concerns about work, health or relationships, or as another 2 a.m. YouTube rabbit hole about how we don't see baby pigeons because all pigeons have cameras in their eyes and are actually spies working for the government and big corporations. Basically, this fear can easily feed back into the other three fears. Anxiety often stems from the fear of the unknown, as we want to control a future situation which, in the present moment, isn't within our control.

The five F's

Just as we can categorise most fears into each of the primal fears we just discussed, we can group our responses to those fears in five different ways as well. These are commonly referred to as the five F's: flight, fight, freeze, flop and fawn. But what goes on when we experience one or more of these responses? And how do they present themselves? Let me use the joyous and camp world of musical theatre to help me explain in further detail. I'm sure you will see yourself in one or more of these stories.

The flight response: Our ability to run ... hopefully very fast. This is when adrenaline (our stress response) rushes through the body because there is immediate danger. This response was useful when we were being stared down by a ravenous sabre-toothed tiger, who's quite literally salivating at the thought of getting his overgrown fangs stuck into us for dinner. That might sound ridiculous now, but we still have modern threats to life and limb, including people who might threaten our physical safety (like muggers), violent weather or oncoming traffic. However it's triggered, the flight response is there to get us away as fast as we can to save ourselves and those we love most.

Like many of you, I've experienced the flight response. As you've probably established, I've often had an intense fear about my performances. Generally, it's about vocal perfectionism and the fear of failure if I'm not perfect. What I used to do when I felt this overwhelming feeling is run. I would run as fast as I could away from opportunities that would evoke that fear. There were several times early in my career when I was asked to sing live on TV. These opportunities were avoided at all costs to avoid public humiliation that would wind up on YouTube or social media forever. I would say no when asked or not reply to the email for a while, hoping they would have asked someone else by the time I got back to them. It took me a long time and a lot of courage to finally overcome that fear. Now you can find a healthy dose of my performances on YouTube where I stuff up, and I bloody love it and am happy to celebrate it. A favourite is slaughtering the 'be' or the high A flat during a performance of 'Music of the Night' in London. I'm sure I was sick that night, but god it's good to have that messy, imperfect and very funny stuff out there.

The fight response: This is similar to 'flight' but, rather than running away, we are facing our threat head-on and fighting it. Disclaimer: I do not recommend fighting a sabre-toothed tiger under any circumstance. It's incredibly unlikely to work out well for you. But there have been many times in my career where I've been scared shitless onstage and have had to grit my teeth, tense my body and fight my way through a show. Whether it's basic worrying, crippling anxiety, being physically unwell or vocally exhausted, the feeling of fighting is terrifying. I can't stand these shows, and I generally crash hard after them.

I remember starting out as the Phantom in London, waiting behind Christine Daaé's dressing room mirror for my first vocal line – maybe you've experienced this prior to a job interview or public speaking. My heart would pound like crazy with nerves and anxiety. For a while, I tried to just keep still, push the feeling away or suppress it. That never worked. Then I would try to breathe deeply and calm myself, which worked sometimes but sort of killed the intensity needed for the Phantom's opening line of 'Insolent boy!' In the end, the only way to stop that fight response from being debilitating was to use it – use my pounding heart as the character's pounding heart. The woman I've fallen for, my muse and my obsession, is being wooed by another man. If that doesn't make your heart pound and your blood boil, nothing will. Leaning into this fear helped me overcome it, and now I get excited rather than terrified. Over the years, I've learned suppression never works for me – leaning into the feeling, even if it's ugly and uncomfortable, always serves me better. Emotions are energy in motion. They have to escape somehow.

The freeze response: This is when we are met with fear and feel temporarily paralysed. Rather than fighting our way through it or running away from it, we are totally stuck, tongue-tied, numb and immobile. Seizing up before or during an important moment is a pretty common response for a lot of people and makes scary moments even scarier.

I had a mega freeze response moment while performing the role of Corny Collins in the UK tour of *Hairspray*. My mental health wasn't great, and I was struggling through anxiety. For those who don't know, Corny is the host of a kids' dance show and has a bunch of monologues effectively down the barrel of the camera. One monologue started with, 'Hey there, guys and gidgets ...' (it's a musical, of course it did). On this particular occasion, I froze for thirty seconds, which was how long the monologue took. Fortunately, a compassionate bunch of the younger cast members, who were equally frozen in front of me, thankfully with perfect showbiz smiles, could feel my anxiety and helped me with my next line, which got me back on track. I felt shit about it for the whole week and, rather than putting it to bed and letting it go, it only made my anxiety increase as I felt the fear of it all happening again. With very limited knowledge of how to tackle this, I spent a fair bit of time white-knuckling some future performances, fighting my way through them until the end of the run in that city. I used the few days between towns as a circuit breaker, but I don't think it ever really worked. Although I didn't have another big freeze moment, I was often on edge during that part of the show. This isn't uncommon for people in long-running shows. Repetition does funny things to us. Lucy Maunder discusses this on season one, episode two of the BTM podcast – she experienced a one-off moment onstage where her ears went crazy to the point she couldn't hear the key. This led to her singing a long, sustained note in the wrong key and a series of panicked moments in the subsequent shows. She learned through therapy that rather than trying to stop the feeling, 'accepting it and thanking (her) body for trying to save (her)' was the best remedy.

The fawn response: This is when we placate or 'people please'. This might be to quash a conflict before it happens, but often we put our own happiness aside to ensure someone else isn't unhappy. We see this in abusive relationships, in friendships, at home and in workplaces, where people are walking on eggshells, too afraid to speak up, speak out or even speak at all. We all want to be liked, I think that's pretty human, but have you ever given up your happiness to try and make another person happy?

For much of my career, I was a people pleaser. I like to be liked and, when someone didn't seem to like me at work, wow, did that make for some serious fawning. I had a hell of a hard time on one show with a particular cast member and spent the entire contract wanting them to like me. It created a really toxic power imbalance, and I became highly anxious about our encounters on- and offstage. Some of it was their fault for behaving awfully, but some was mine for not having strong enough boundaries and enabling their behaviour. This situation taught me a valuable lesson about how destructive the fawn response can be, and I've had to learn the hard way, many times over, that you can be kind and warm and still have very clear boundaries.

The flop response: This is when we are too overwhelmed for a physical or mental response and may even faint. It's what happens when we are completely overwhelmed by our circumstances and we basically can't respond. Have you ever been so fearful you've fainted, fallen ill or something similar before a big moment in your life?

I've never fainted, but I have certainly flopped in terms of illness and burnout, both due to stress and fear. This has happened countless times in my career, usually when approaching something important or when stress is getting the better of me. It causes me pain, disappointment, frustration and a loss of income when it happens, and I've had to reflect on which of those occurrences are simply bad luck and which ones I've played my role in.

Ultimately though, fear is inherently part of the human experience – we need it or we wouldn't survive very long. What's important to note is that while we don't get to choose what we find frightening, we do get to choose how we respond to that fear.

I didn't look like them

The way we communicate with or judge ourselves plays a huge part in all this. Our ego loves to judge. The authentic self, the soul, doesn't judge. Self-judgement is something we all struggle with, and self-love is something we can all work on. Self-love is just a simple way of describing kindness, grace and compassion for ourselves. It's about letting go of the idea that our worth is dependent on anyone else's opinion of us. It's removing expectations of perfection and celebrating ourselves, shifting our mindset so that our inner critic becomes our inner champion rather than continually reinforcing the fear that we are not enough.

As you can tell, I've had some fairly serious 'not enough' stories throughout my life. They tie into my fear of abandonment, of not being valued, respected, seen, heard or validated. I'm not alone there. I have healed some of the traumas that have manifested from this fear, and some I'm still working through. Aside from my craft as a performer, the major one I've tackled is body image. I had never opened up publicly about this until discussing it briefly in season two, episode fourteen of the BTM podcast with Megan Waters and Duncan McDaide. It has been a shame I have sat with silently for years, but I want to draw light to the stigma around body image for young men. The more we talk about the issues of body shaming and the expectations society puts on everyone to aspire towards 'the perfect' aesthetic, the more we work to heal individually and systemically.

Growing up, I never had big problems with my weight, but I wasn't one of those skin-and-bones kids who had a sixpack regardless of how many packets of Pizza Shapes or bottles of Coke they inhaled. My first recollection of being body conscious was at swimming sports in year 5. I was comparing my body to some of the more athletic boys and felt shit that mine didn't look like theirs. My body went in at the shoulders and out at the waist, and theirs did the opposite. In my head, they looked like young Greek gods, and I, well ... I just thought I looked like shit.

This feeling of aesthetic inadequacy only grew throughout high school. I started puberty a fair bit later than most guys and hung onto my puppy fat, so in those awkward years between twelve and fifteen, I was bullied by some of the more physically advanced boys. They called me a tubby little Jewboy when they saw the cellulite on my stomach in the change rooms. I didn't know why, but I hated it and I hated them for making me feel even shittier. Sticks and stones aside, I had never been bullied at primary school, but I have always been very sensitive, and names hurt me a lot. (That old wound.) By the time school ended, I'd had my growth spurt and lengthened out a bit. But while the puppy fat had gone, the feeling of inadequacy hadn't.

At university, I started to expand outwards again, so I decided to get fit and lose the weight. I had to take control. My belief was that musical theatre was for men with perfect bodies, and I wasn't stepping out into the musical theatre industry at the end of third year and not looking a million bucks. In three and a half months, I lost over ten kilograms by cutting out carbs and running around Albert Park Lake (Melbourne's Grand Prix track) almost every day. Each day, I would weigh myself and look at myself in the mirror to check where the fat was. I had to get rid of it.

When I got back to uni for the start of third year, I had abs for the first time. I was lean and fit, and people were commenting on how good I looked. That fed my ego to no end. It reaffirmed to me that if I look good, people will treat me nicely and won't bully me. No tubby little Jewboy here. I had found a new mask to wear – the lean, fit dude mask. My lecturers said I had to put on some more muscle to play the lead role at the end of the year so, although I kept up the running, I started going to the gym and drinking protein shakes – real 20-year-old bloke stuff! This only fuelled the toxic relationship I had with my physical appearance.

For the years following, I yoyoed between looking relatively fit and being absolutely ripped. I would get obsessive for a while, create an extreme change in my diet and training regimen, work out like a madman in the most unsustainable ways, get to a point where I thought I looked amazing (and was equally exhausted) and then crash, both with training and diet. I would binge-diet and starve myself. Then, if I had the tiniest bit of junk food, I would say to myself, 'You fucked it. Righto, you're off the wagon,' and guilt-eat everything I could get my hands on. I would eat chips, chocolate, ice cream, burgers, pizzas, all in one sitting, just to fill up on what I had been craving and depriving myself of. To this day, I don't keep certain foods in the cupboard because I've learned not to trust myself with them.

There's no doubt I felt an inadequacy, a deep not-enoughness and, by the time I was performing in *An Officer and a Gentleman* in 2012, my anxiety around my body image was at an all-time high. As a cast we were all in extraordinary shape, me included, but I would look at the bodies of the other ripped guys and compare myself to them from the lens of a tubby Jewboy and feel like an imposter.

It also played deeply into a perfectionist construct I had built for myself. I was so scared that my love handles would come back – it didn't help when one of the creative team requested that I 'watch the muffin top' at a topless photoshoot for the show. After that, the bulimia set in. I started throwing up after meals and took cutting pills (high doses of caffeine) to help me stay lean. I was offered fitness modelling opportunities at that time, appearing in *Men's Health* magazine, an exhausted shell of a human but apparently 'aesthetically aspirational'. I was so caught up with how I looked that it didn't even occur to me that tripping over a high set piece during a performance, which resulted in a concussion and hospitalisation, might have had something to do with what I was putting in my body (or not putting in it) and what I was throwing up.

After that episode, for at least a year I still had problems with body image and bulimia. I got very good at hiding that, sneaking off to the bathroom after meals or when I was out with friends at bars or clubs. I was good at hiding the shame I felt around my actions. I knew I couldn't sustain this, and I hated the person I was becoming more than I hated not looking a certain way. So, I studied to become a personal trainer. In that time and the subsequent years working in the fitness business, I was educated on more sustainable science around training and eating so I could be in better shape more consistently and not yoyo as much.

However, it didn't stop the deep-seated feeling of not-enoughness. That's taken me many years of being brave and honest with myself, of therapy, of reflection and going inward and really asking why I feel a need to look a certain way to feel like I'm enough. I've looked that tubby little Jewboy in the eyes, hugged him and told him he's beautiful just the way he is. I've cried through some tough answers around a need for validation and love and, as I've done that, my relationship with fitness and my body has changed for the better.

There have been times where I've fallen back into old mindsets and patterns, certainly not as extreme as the *Officer and Gentleman* moments. Although challenging, reflection got me to a point where I like to train to feel good – I like to challenge myself without ever being extreme – I vary my training (a mix of gym, running and yoga) and enjoy taking care of my body in conjunction with my mind and soul. I like to nourish my body with unprocessed food as much as possible to help me feel more balanced throughout the day and to sleep better. There's a relaxed discipline to it, and I still believe that discipline is one of the greatest, and most overlooked, acts of self-love. It says that I value my relationship with myself and I want to foster that relationship to help it to grow. It also says I'm going to relinquish what I want right now for what I really want in the future.

I'm also a firm believer in creating harmony and balance in all parts of life: food and exercise included. Balance is integral to ensuring the world and everything in it operates smoothly. It has taken me a long time to really learn that. So, as much as I value healthy food and regular exercise, I also love a couple of cheeky spicy margys and a few mouth-watering tacos, or a glass or two of red with my delicious capriccioso pizza, and that's bloody great too.

In this particular instance, I'm glad I saw a psychologist and discussed this with them. This was something I couldn't fully tackle alone and I found talk therapy really helpful for addressing my fear of not being enough unless I looked a certain way. I worked through this over many sessions, but it's also taken time to shift, and I've learned the patterns and how to catch myself if and when old patterns or that critical voice re-emerge.

Do I look the way I did ten years ago? God no. Am I generally happier? I know so, and feel so, and that's about the only validation I need. Thankfully, it doesn't need to come from anybody but myself and, in lowering the previously lofty standards of my own expectations, I've reduced the deafening volume of my inner critic, which has helped me to continue to love myself.

Your relationship with fear

Fear and I have had an interesting and complex relationship since I began performing. I've suppressed it, hated it, faced it and later learned that I have to love it. I'm sure your relationship with fear is just as interesting if you look at it. In an interview, one of my all-time favourite singers, the late, great Pavarotti, once said, 'Every moment you go onstage, you must be scared. If you are not scared, you are not an artist.' I firmly agree with him, but there's a difference between being a bit scared or jittery and legitimately shitting yourself. Believe me, in my early days playing Tony in *West Side Story*, there wasn't a show I did without spending at least five or ten minutes on the toilet before going onstage. I was *that* scared, and my stomach knew all about it. It took me a while to learn that to break through the fear cycle, I had to lean into the fear rather than responding with one of the five Fs.

It is also important to acknowledge that we live in a world where some individuals and groups are *permanently* dealing with real existential or violent threats, sometimes daily. Not everyone has the luxury of perspective or control over their circumstances. For people dealing with these threats and fears, these fear responses are vital for survival.

Modern living exposes physical and chemical reactions to events that aren't served by these stress responses. There is no violent conflict or existential threat, yet we respond as if that is the case: traffic jams, public speaking, uncomfortable conversations, meeting the in-laws for the first time, getting the kids to school in the morning, that triggering Instagram post ... argh! These all play into our fears, but our response to them is having a profoundly detrimental effect on our physical, mental and emotional health. Our fear responses are being triggered constantly. When we operate in this state long term, we are far more reactive and less capable of more helpful responses to difficulties in our life. We are more easily agitated, more anxious and aggressive, more stressed and less focused. It negatively impacts our relationships, our working environment and our experience of life. It's actually making us sick.

Part of learning to be comfortable with fear is understanding what makes us afraid, then working out appropriate responses to it. Sometimes this is about responding better to the stressor, but other times this is learning to cut negative things out of our lives. We also have to be very aware of the power of disinformation and misinformation and the effect that's having on our fear response. As Liberal MP Zoe McKenzie says in season two, episode four of the BTM podcast, 'Do you honestly think what you're reading on social media is free? It's algorithmically perverted. You are getting fed the nasty stuff, the sizzle, the stuff that's designed to make you react.' Often, that reaction is a fear response. And our dopamine addictions to our smartphones cause us to stay on these platforms for hours even if they are exacerbating that fear response. I have actually installed an app blocker so I can't mindlessly scroll through social media. It has been the most effective way to reduce phone time and cut something negative out of my life. Social media doesn't help me become a better human, and I would argue that much of our inability to listen to each other and have healthy discussions and disagreements is because of social media.

The thing about the sizzle and nastiness on social media is that it creates a false fear. We are reacting as if we are experiencing that racism, that tragedy, that violence, that war, when really we're safely in our homes on the couch, sitting in a café or on public transport. It's not in tune with the present moment. Yes, we need to be aware of what's happening in the world and not have our head in the sand, but overexposure to this sort of stuff is detrimental to our health and creates false fear. These aren't limited to social media – we have countless false fears in our lives, which usually come back to one of the four primal fears and ultimately diminish our capacity to live fully.

At some stage in our lives, once we acknowledge the false prison we are in, we can make a conscious choice to step into the fire of our fears. We've acknowledged that things can be bloody scary, but also that we can respond in a different way. We can't let fear limit us from exploring our full potential as humans. This takes courage, vulnerability and probably a few tears. Sometimes, it's consciously deciding to seek and embrace discomfort through a series of consistently small moments, giving us the confidence to tackle more challenging moments incrementally. Other times, the universe, in its infinite, sadistic wisdom, bestows a huge challenge or crisis upon us and we can either step into one of the five F's and repeat a cycle we are in, or we can tackle this fear beast head-on.

Life doesn't owe us anything but it *is* here to challenge us. Sticky and crunchy situations are inevitable, and it's in the moments of extreme discomfort, adversity and crisis where we learn the most about ourselves and grow. We see this with athletes and performers all the time, where the magnitude of the moment evokes a superhuman response. We see it in life-threatening rescues completed by our day-to-day emergency service heroes ... and we see in it ourselves when we bravely dive into 'the work'. Fear is our opportunity for growth, if we have the courage to face it. Fear is also inevitable; courage, however, is optional.

Stepping into the fire

As I've said, I've always had a fear of singing solo on live TV.

I'd had a couple of opportunities to sing on TV earlier that I had either run away from (flight) or that I had missed due to falling ill as the opportunity approached (flopped). In 2017, I recorded an album with musician, producer, conductor and now long-time friend John Foreman. It was an album of pop tunes reworked in a classical style – feel free to stop reading and go check it out on Spotify. Track six, 'Say Something', is my personal fave!

In 2018, I had just finished doing eight shows a week for a year playing Gerry Goffin in *Beautiful: The Carole King Musical.* I was on holiday in Tuscany, Italy, when I got a call from John. After the usual small talk, which normally consists of John making me laugh – he's one of the funniest people you'll ever meet – he drops a bomb on me.

'So, the Australia Day Live concert is coming up. It takes place on the forecourt of the Sydney Opera House and is nationally broadcast on the ABC. It's a pop/rock concert celebrating Australian artists, but each year we do a homage to the Opera House where someone performs an aria, and we'd like you to sing "Nessun Dorma". Would you be interested?' I was immediately met with a rush of adrenaline. Every part of me froze. I was momentarily lost for words. To this day, I don't know how or why I said yes when all the fear inside me wanted to say no, but 'yes' came out of my mouth, and I'm forever grateful it did. It was the firecracker I needed personally and professionally.

After coming to terms with the idea that this was actually happening, I decided, like I often do, to get down to work and started practising daily and working with my singing coach on it. I had sung it at different times in my career but nothing like this, and I wanted to fine-tune it for my voice. I also hoped that with potentially millions of eyes on me and nerves going through the roof, my muscle memory would kick in and I could be grounded in that. We're not whipping out some Rick Astley at late-night karaoke here – this is 'Nessun "fuckin" Dorma', arguably the most iconic aria and certainly the most recognisable. It requires an immense amount of technique and detail and an equal amount of passion. In the lead-up, I had moments of feeling ill with fear just thinking about it, but then, as my confidence grew and I felt really comfortable with how I was singing it technically, the fear began to wash away. I got back to what lights me up and focused on sharing this powerful piece, the passion and love it required, and it made me feel powerful and excited about the opportunity to share my version of it. It was a clear reminder that discipline and diligence in practice builds our confidence.

Sitting in my dressing room in the Opera House on Australia Day, looking at all the people on the Harbour and visualising exactly how the performance was going to go, I was a far cry from the person who answered that phone call back in October. Those three months of dedication stood me in great stead because, to this day, it's one of my favourite performances. I'll forever be proud of it. Towards the end of the song, I recall feeling a wave of bliss rush over me, unlike anything I had felt onstage before. I recall looking out on that sea of people and the Sydney Opera House behind them and thinking, 'Holy fuck, this is my life, how bloody awesome!' Singing that soaring top note at the end was like purging all the years of fear out of me.

I conquered something very big that night, a huge fear of public failure, and I know that leaning into that discomfort and stepping through that fire helped me to expand both as an artist and a person like nothing had before. I'm forever grateful to John for asking me to perform and offering me an opportunity to truly embrace and face my fears, and for always believing in me, even when I didn't fully believe in myself. We all need people like that in our lives – mentors, coaches, champions and supporters who lift us up and make our inner fire burn fiercely. John has been that for me for almost fifteen years. I appreciate him so much – I know that my life would be very different without him in it.

Learning to be uncomfortable

I highly recommend finding ways to really sit in discomfort. Over the years, I've challenged myself to do it often to build and train resilience in all parts of my life. Whether physical, mental or emotional, we learn more about ourselves in discomfort than when life is cruising in fifth gear down Easy Street. There are lots of ways to do this, but basically anything that pushes us beyond our comfort zone will do the trick. It might be an open, confronting conversation with a friend, partner or work colleague where you have to be vulnerable enough to admit your flaws and shortcomings. It might be one where you are brave enough to call someone else out on their poor behaviour because it doesn't align with your values or the organisation's, even if that means losing your job, lover or friend. Maybe it's pushing your body through immense physical exertion, beyond your perceived limitations, or sitting still in meditation if you're always moving, hiking up a mountain if you're afraid of heights, or trying something new, like taking all your clothes off and jumping into freezing cold water.

There has been a lot of noise about ice bathing. Is it just a crock of bollocks that social media influencers get into as another excuse to get the abs out, or is it actually rooted in science? Either way, I assure you it evokes a fierce wave of discomfort for most people, me included, so I recommend subjecting yourself to the experience as an exercise in building resilience.

I got into ice baths (pun absolutely intended) in 2018. I was performing in *Beautiful: The Carole King Musical*, and was struggling with anxiety. Asher, a qualified instructor, was running a workshop at a fitness studio I owned at the time and invited me to attend. Now, I wasn't one to even take cold showers at that stage of my life, other than the occasional hot-and-cold shower to move some lactic acid after the annual charity Theatre Footy Day, which always left me broken and bruised (thespians chasséing around the footy oval – butch, I know), so the thought of jumping into an ice bath was incredibly overwhelming. Asher, probably sensing I was having a challenging time at work, convinced me to go along for the ride. And what a ride it was. This wasn't just a cold-water plunge – this was a baby pool filled to the brim with packet after packet of thick ice cubes. It was equal parts intimidating and freezing!

With adrenaline dancing through our bodies like a group of teens pinging off their heads at a rave, and the room heavy with the collective anxiety of the twenty-plus shit-scared participants, I figured it was best not to wait any longer than necessary and threw myself into the first small group of prospective plungers. Now, I knew it was going to be uncomfortable, and I could feel my heart racing as I went to step in, but nothing can adequately prepare you for your ice bath debut – it's a very different kind of frozen. Like fuck off, Elsa, the cold is absolutely bothering me in EVERY WAY!

As I submerged myself in the ice, I tried to close my eyes and, with Asher's guidance, focus purely on my breath. As I was basically hyperventilating, I realised fairly quickly that I had three options. Every part of me wanted to escape, to run back to comfort, to a soft fluffy towel that had just come out of the dryer or, better yet, a cosy campfire with some marshmallow skewers. Oh, hello flight option, don't you look cute right now. But I had to endure only three minutes ... surely I could do that. Flight was no longer an option.

Option two was to fight. To grit my way through it, clench every muscle: my jaw, hands, feet, teeth and toes, even my sphincter (yeah, I went there). That'll work for three minutes – just grind it out, sphincter and all. But then it occurred to me that that's what I had been doing onstage for the past six or so months, and that wasn't working for me. Maybe there was another option that would help me through the rest of this contract.

Enter option three. As I sat there with my breath, my mind began to shift away from the fierce cold and the intrusive thoughts and, after a minute and a half, I just let go. I surrendered to the experience, and the strangest thing happened – the parts of my body submerged in the cold felt warmer than the ones out of the water. Euphoria had set in. In the ice, in the surrender, I found so much calm, so much freedom, so much beauty. Since then, I have sat in hundreds of ice baths – few have been as life-changing as that one, but all of them remind me of the power of surrender.

I hope this inspires you to jump into an ice bath. But, if that's too much for you, start with a ten-second cold shower and increase it by ten seconds each day. Notice how it makes you feel – the discomfort, the struggle, the fight, the flight or maybe (if you focus purely on breathing calmly in and out of your nose, elongating the breath) the surrender. Also notice how alive you feel after the shower. That dopamine kick is epic, and you're expanding your resilience. Once you hit two minutes, you're ready for the ice.

Exercise: overcoming discomfort visualisation

There are countless actions you can take immediately to build your resilience and confidence to feel less fear and more freedom. This is a three-minute exercise I use to help me tackle discomfort mentally before facing it in the real world.

Start by writing down something that you fear or causes you discomfort. It could be small or large – something that has been agitating, frustrating, upsetting or challenging you for some time. If you haven't met this fear head-on, you're likely to be resisting it or pushing it away somehow. What we resist persists and tends to come back more fiercely, so by taking steps to move beyond fear, you're also taking the first step to avoid resistance.

Now, close your eyes and meditate on this discomfort for the next few minutes. Visualise yourself in the same space as that fear – whatever is triggering your discomfort is right there, facing you. Notice the feelings it brings up for you. Rather than stopping those feelings or running away from them, really lean into them and feel them all – the struggle, the anger, the pain, the shame, the anguish, the unrest, agitation ... whatever those feelings and emotions are, just be with them. Remember that emotions are energy in motion – they have to move. Give them permission to do so.

Now envisage yourself taking on that fear, tackling it calmly and confidently with an easy, grounded focus. Imagine yourself surrendering to the moment and prevailing through the discomfort, and notice how that makes you feel. Is it elated, relieved, excited, free, seen, calm, heard, proud, loved?

When you feel ready, take a big breath in through your

nose into your belly, ribs and chest, then open your mouth and audibly sigh out everything you're holding on to. Feel free to do that a couple more times.

Now open your eyes, put procrastination to one side and tackle your fears. Feel the fear and do it anyway. Although not everything in life is going to go perfectly or go our way, by taking action, we give ourselves the best possible opportunity to build our resilience and relax into surrender.

Don't suffer twice

Injuries and illness are a normal part of anyone's life, the latter especially for performers, but they can be incredibly frustrating and cause anxiety and discomfort, especially if they happen ahead of a big performance. At the start of my contract to play Jean Valjean in *Les Misérables* in London, I had one of the nastiest injuries a singer could think of, a fracture to the left posterior side of my thyroid cartilage – the back of my voice box.

It happened on day three of rehearsals during 'The Confrontation' between Javert and Valjean, which is their fight scene. Through a series of unlucky events, I was struck in the throat by my fellow actor's forearm, which jammed my larynx against the back of my neck. Hideous, I know! I pushed through the rest of the rehearsal with the pain masked by a ton of adrenaline. I knew something was wrong when I cooled down an hour or so later and was still in excruciating pain. I spent that evening in the emergency ward. After sitting there for five or six hours (bloody NHS), I decided it was best to go home and see the specialist the next day.

After a consultation, some scans and a few days of painkillers, I got the news about the scale of the injury. A fractured thyroid cartilage. It required four to six weeks of recovery, and ten days with no talking. I wasn't even in shock. I could barely talk or swallow without agony, so the call only confirmed what I thought had happened. I was grateful that it wasn't a worst-case scenario – apparently it was a centimetre or so away from a six-to-nine-month recovery or potentially never being able to sing again. Anyway, the ten days of no talking was like doing a Vipassana (silent retreat) at home, which I had been keen to do for some time, so there was a silver lining there. The repercussion was that my opening night would be delayed a month or so and, in the scheme of one's life, that wasn't such a big deal.

I had been working for twenty years to get to this point in my career – there were a bunch of paths my thoughts could've gone down. What if my voice never fully recovered? What if I lost my range and could no longer sing the role? I swear, if I hadn't meditated for years prior and at least an hour each day in those first ten days, I could've gone down a very woe-is-me, victim-mindset path – what the yogis call the path of the second suffering.

The first suffering was the blow, which was out of my control. The second suffering we often choose is the suffering of the mind, where we lose our capacity for discernment and let our thoughts dictate our emotions and feelings. As I sat there reflecting and meditating upon what had happened, and what it really meant, I was reminded again and again of impermanence – 'This too shall pass'.

Nothing is forever. That beautiful holiday, that frustrating conflict, that corrupt government, that traffic jam, that annoyingly successful football team, that painfully unsuccessful one, Covid lockdowns, opening nights, that nasty throat injury, they all come and go. Everything has its season. Sure, there were moments of feeling disappointed, frustrated, concerned or upset. I sat with them all, watching them pass as well and, by the time my opening night came five weeks later, it was worth every second of the wait. The recovery process had given me time to think more deeply about the role, to acknowledge the gratitude I had for the opportunity, to get to know the wonderful people in the cast and crew and to savour the sweetness of that opening night. It's a richer ride when we've travelled through adversity to our destination. The richness of that first performance is something I'll never forget. 'This too shall pass' was such a powerful mantra. When there was every possibility of drowning in fear, dread, stress or anxiety, this enabled me to stay calm, to have a sense of confidence about the future and to stay grounded in the present.

Journal exercise: reflecting on reactions

Ask yourself: When was the last serious illness or injury you had? When was the last time you got bogged down in reacting to something that was quite clearly only going to affect you temporarily? What is your relationship with your own internal suffering? How did you react or respond to it? How would that have changed if you had reminded yourself that 'This too shall pass'?

Write your answers and thoughts down. You can also use your journal to reflect on new obstacles to remind yourself that this is only temporary.

The feather, the brick and the train

Unfortunately, the adversity during *Les Misérables* didn't end there. Of course, there were illnesses and battling through the weekly grind, aiming to perform such a challenging role seven times a week off the back of a fairly serious injury to the most important part of a singer's anatomy. It took me about six or so weeks into the run before my voice began to feel like it had prior to the injury. I had probably gone back a bit too early or bitten off more than I could chew too quickly with the number of shows, but by mid-year I felt settled and in command of the role.

For a few months, I felt like I was soaring. There is nothing more rewarding or fulfilling than feeling free in a role as expansive and robust as Jean Valjean. It's the most astonishing onstage marathon I have endured. As word got around that I had really found my groove, the creative team and producers (including Cameron Mackintosh) came to see me perform, and I was offered a new contract. I was weighing it all up as my father was having some heart troubles at the time, but after a successful surgery, he informed me he was A-OK and I signed on for a further five months. This was the dream job, the one I had worked two decades for. I figured another five months would square the ledger.

How wrong I was. On a mid-season break in Portugal, I got a call from my parents with the devastating news that my father had been diagnosed with brain cancer. It shattered me. As focused and resilient as my mind had been, on a deeper level I was clearly exhausted, hanging on by a thread. My nervous system was shot – I was running most days on pure adrenaline, bordering on full-blown burnout, and this news tipped me over the edge. Shows became virtually impossible for me to do. I would go out there and bawl my eyes out, especially during songs like 'Bring Him Home'. All I wanted to do was bring myself home to be with him.

At this time, I recalled one of the great theories Asher had taught me: the feather, the brick and the train. The idea is that when the universe wants you to listen, it will first brush you gently with a feather. I think my feather came before I started at *Les Misérables*. There was about a week between finishing the run of *The Phantom of the Opera* in

Melbourne and getting to London to start *Les Mis* rehearsals. I was already mentally tired after the eight-month *Phantom* run and could've used a month's break to put some petrol in the tank. Unfortunately, I didn't have the courage to communicate that with the *Les Mis* producers at the time. I was afraid I wouldn't be allowed to do the role on those terms, so I rocked up to London unrested.

Next is the brick, which hits you pretty hard. Well, I think the injury to the throat was pretty damn brickish! Maybe I should have listened more closely and taken some more serious time out. Maybe the universe was asking me to do this, and I just couldn't see it. But people get hit with bricks all the time, adversity is a part of life, so I thought maybe the universe was testing me or simply reminding me that this too shall pass. It also technically gave me the month-long break I was after, just not as I had envisaged.

Then there's the train, something so big and powerful that, when it hits you, it flattens you and you have no option but to stop everything. Put your foot on the brakes, turn off the engine, get the hell out of the car. This was my train moment. Dad was suffering back home, and here I was breaking down in London, incapable of doing my job properly. *Playing* a dying father was just too much for me.

There were times during *Les Mis* where I looked at myself in the mirror of my dressing room and saw strength, courage, resilience and fire. Other times, I saw a fraud, a fake and shameful imposter and a failure. Other times, I saw the boy who dreamed this whole thing up twenty years earlier. But, when the news about my dad hit, it was like I was looking through the mirror into empty space. I couldn't see my reflection; it felt like I wasn't supposed to be there. I knew that the only way forward was to leave that dressing room altogether. The universe had hit me with the triple combo: mental fatigue, a physical injury and now a painful emotional one. I was completely and utterly cooked. This choice didn't spark any fear within me. Family is family. There's no rationale needed. It's just more important than anything, including my career.

I spoke to my management back home and the team at Cameron Mackintosh Ltd, and I eventually decided it was best to finish up at *Les Mis*, go home and be with my family. When I called to tell them, my dad broke down with tears of relief. Both of my parents knew how much this role meant to me and would never ask me to choose them over the opportunity, but for me there was no choice. The pain of not being there with him was far greater than the desire to be out there performing, and they were so grateful I made the choice I did.

The relief I felt getting on that plane and flying home was a huge weight off my shoulders. Seeing Dad was both beautiful and emotional. As the months have progressed, thankfully his condition has remained stable. Being with my family was the best decision I ever made, for my physical and mental state, and for them. It's a decision I'll never, ever regret. I've learned that sometimes in life, there are powers bigger than us at play and, no matter how much you want something in your head and heart, it's just not meant to be. Even when you're at the top, looking after yourself and caring for your family is more important than anything. Hopefully I learn to listen more intently and respond to the feathers rather than waiting for the train.

Train crashes can echo

Ironically enough, the day I decided I was going to leave the show early, I caught the train to Bristol to go to one of those man-made surf parks. On my second surf lesson of the day, I wiped-out and was struck by my surfboard, once again in the throat. You might call it two trains colliding, making sure I didn't ignore things anymore. Through an intense course of corticosteroids, I got back for one last show of *Les Misérables* but, unlike my first injury, this one forced me to completely stop for a long time, then go very slowly through vocal rehabilitation and recovery.

The blow damaged the nerves that help the movement and functionality of the cricothyroid muscle, the one responsible for the stretching and tilting of the larynx ... in other words, the one that makes you sing well. My left vocal cord was now unable to meet the right in certain places, leading to the immense difficulty of doing something that was second nature to me.

With no case studies for an injury as specific as this to

a singer, I spent many months with two steps forward, two steps back, trying to get the answers, trying to work out how on earth I was going to sing again. There were days where the nerves would fire and I magically could sing, and many, many more infuriating days where my voice simply wouldn't work. Unlike the first injury, which had a linear road to recovery that helped me find peace and perspective relatively easily, this has had many ups and downs.

With all that had happened in the previous months: the sadness of my father's cancer, the pain of leaving my dream job, and now not being able to do the thing I loved most, I finally broke. Even with all the self and spiritual work I had done, I was not invincible. I couldn't deal with it – I had to drop my mask, the one that says I've got it sorted, because I didn't. The fear my voice would never work properly again was too strong for me and, in many ways, I began a process of crumbling and grieving.

I went through the stages of grief: denial, anger, bargaining, depression and acceptance. In a 2024 interview, the great Canadian actor and comedian Jim Carey once repeated something that his spiritual friend Jeff Foster had told him about depression: 'Think of depressed as deep rest ... your body needs deep rest from the characters you're trying to play.' I had been playing some pretty big ones since the world had opened up from lockdowns.

I lay in that deep rest for some time, but also sought the help I needed. I worked with a team of great supportive people: a psychologist; my voice pathologist, Dr Debbie Phyland; ENT specialist Dr Catherine Sinc; a physiotherapist: a Feldenkrais practitioner, an energy healer and a reiki therapist; and had many sessions with singing coaches, all combining together to crack the code of rehab and recovery. Finally, after controlling all I could control for as long as I could, the best course of action was intervention. In May 2024, and again in August 2024, I had surgeries on my left vocal cord to fill it with Juvéderm, a filler. Yeah, I've had my little shot of bobo, and I'm proud of it! It helps my left cord to meet my right one, and over time it has worked.

Is my voice back to exactly what it was pre-injury? No, but it's not far off and I'm working towards it every day. Am I sad about it all? I am sometimes, and sometimes I'm truly grateful. I see that there's a bigger teacher in all of this and there is no better teaching than suffering. The journey through these challenging, frustrating and agonisingly painful times taught me a lot of important lessons ... what's more, I'm grateful that I *can* sing again. It could have been a lot worse. With rehab, my voice continues to improve in all the subtle ways that a singer notices – I'm sure that I sound exactly the same to a lot of people!

I guess this is goodbye ... for now

Looking back, there were days when I felt strong and days when I was crying in the foetal position on my living room floor. Days when I was numb. Days when I was angry. Days when I resented the career I had chosen and blamed people in positions of power at Cameron Mackintosh Ltd, and days when I owned it all, every aspect of every choice I made and didn't make, every word I uttered and didn't utter, every boundary I enforced and the many I broke. There were days when I could surrender and days when I wanted to control and force it all to work again. Ultimately, I had to come to terms with the possibility of a death, an ending of some sort, that my voice would never be the way it had been.

That's when I started to come out the other side. As is so often the case, it's in the darkness that we truly begin to see the light clearly. This period of time rendered me unable to wear my singing mask, so I had to spend more time being Josh the nobody. It was a firm reminder that I alone am enough. It also helped me to recognise that I'm not alone in this – there are many people out there, performers or otherwise, who are struggling with their voices, literally and figuratively. I chose to be very public with my experience in the hope that it would help performers release the stigma and shame around the imperfections of their voices.

Importantly, this period forced me to reflect on my career. I now know that, beyond just the singing limitations I felt, deep down I don't want to perform in so many big musicals anymore. I've done all I needed to do in that space and learned everything I need to learn for now. Anything else that happens is a bonus. I'm grateful for the experiences, the lessons, the people I've met and worked with, the friends I've made, the stages I've graced and the audiences I've been able to share exquisite stories and songs with. All of it! For so long, I used the characters I played as a vehicle to share what I felt incapable of sharing in real life: my suppressed and repressed emotions. They were, in many ways, therapy or catharsis. Now I feel free to share these things in my day-to-day life and don't feel the need to step into the confines of character to truly express them. This doesn't mean I won't perform in musicals again; I'll just be far more selective. I see this as a completion of a chapter in my life. The book is still being written, and who knows what's to come?

To be honest, I don't always feel my best self when I'm doing a long run of a big musical. Not only does it require immense sacrifices in other parts of my life – family, social, various other creative and charitable pursuits – it can also play into that need for extrinsic validation. That's not always a bad thing, as we need a certain level of that, but at times it's a bit of a prison for my ego. Although I've walked a path of transcending and then loving the ego (sometimes successfully, other times not), the state of exhaustion, adrenal fatigue and fierce isolation I feel when performing roles like the Phantom and Jean Valjean are battles I no longer want to fight. These characters ask so much of me. I spend so many days and shows vocally resting, physically exhausted, just in survival mode, and I find it incredibly difficult to access that divine state I long for onstage, the one that makes sharing art so crucial for our collective hearts. Originally, there was fear in making a decision like this – fears around finance, around what I would do if I wasn't always doing a musical – but I've reconciled those by meditating beyond the noise of my thinking mind and ego, and listened to the bigger voice of true knowing (some people call it intuition or the voice of the heart) which is often much harder to hear, because the noisy ego is drowning it out. When you learn to listen and trust that voice, making brave decisions like this one becomes easier, as ultimately, in your heart of hearts, you know they are right and that they align with your values.

This doesn't mean I won't continue singing. I plan to perform in concerts and create all sorts of varied live performance experiences for artists, such as in public speaking workshops and corporate coaching, for many, many years to come. I realise my calling in this lifetime, in this body, expands beyond the confines of the bright lights of the big commercial musical theatre stage, and I'm excited about the possibilities of serving the world in so many more beautiful, profound and creative ways.

3

PART 3

Awareness

What is awareness?

Once we understand that we are a product of our fears and our reactions to those fears, we can begin to work on our awareness. Most people are asleep at the wheel, just existing in the rat-race of life on a purely physical and psychological level without a relationship with their deeper self.

Earlier, I mentioned that I am 'the awareness', and it all got a bit woo-woo. Now it's time to make sense of all that. Awareness is our deeper or true self. In Hindi it is known as the *atman*, the witness, the observer, consciousness or even the soul. It is formless, timeless and spaceless. It is the one that witnesses all the thoughts, the fears, the judgements, the sufferings, the actions and all the comings and goings of life. It is the self beyond the roles, identities, conditioning and masks we all wear.

Too many of us are trapped in the suffering and identifications of our thinking minds: our egos. The incessant noise, anxieties, worries and conversations in there quite literally do our heads in. Our masks seem rusted on! We are stuck thinking we're the thought, rather than being able to quietly observe those thoughts as the awareness. Expanding the space between the infinite nature of our true self, *the awareness,* and the very narrow nature of our highly reactive thinking minds, gives our lives so much more of the freedom, ease and peace we are searching for. But how do we do that?

Awareness is inherently elusive, because it's interwoven with the state of presence. When we think we've become aware of our awareness, we're actually thinking and, by very definition, we are therefore no longer fully present or aware. Awareness is fully alive in the here and now, not in the future or past. When we form those great memories with people we love, those experiences are always happening in the now. There is only the present moment, and awareness is about establishing ourselves fully and completely in that moment.

As humans, we struggle to sustain the feeling of awareness, mainly because it asks us for surrender. You must surrender to presence – you can't make it happen by controlling it. And needing to control things, whether outcomes, ideas or other people, is one of the biggest issues we tackle as human beings.

Reclaiming our power – the six power P's

We try to control things because we believe we need things to go a certain way for us to be contented. This mindset creates a version of our life that is restrictive, tense and stressful. There is a better way, one that gives us far more agency and power. It also stops us from handing our self-worth over to anyone else. It took me many years to learn this as a performer, but it also applies to any relationship, personal or professional. It's something I like to call 'The six power P's'. These are the things that allow us to control as much as we can in our lives. I use this when working with up-and-coming performing artists and in public-speaking workshops and coaching sessions. It's a wonderful tool.

Preparation: Being prepared is an act of discipline and dedication – real self-love – and this is something we *can* put our focus into. So often we skip over this, wanting to get to the good stuff or get closer to our goal, but giving ourselves adequate time to prepare enables us the best chance of actually getting there. Think of our goal like a tree – preparation is our roots. The more time and energy we carve out to build a vast, deep expanse of strong roots, the more chance we have of growing a solid and strong 'goal tree'. Too many of us are focusing on the branches before building the roots. And, while you might make something that looks like a tree that way, it won't stand the test of time.

Purpose: We all need a clear purpose in life, one that gives us direction and intention. So many people struggle to truly understand purpose – they think it's a career choice or an achievement. But it's far deeper than that, and you'll learn all about it as you work your way through the rest of the book, including where to find it, how to lead and serve with it, and how to impact the world with your unique purpose.

Presence: A lot of fear and anxieties come from the true self being in one place and time while the mind fears its prediction of what may happen in a future place and time. Our struggle with the distance between those two things is responsible for a lot of our internal suffering. Presence creates a focus on the process rather than the outcome and helps you stay in the moment. This requires both trust and acceptance: trust that everything will go as it should, given the preparation you've put in, and acceptance that if it doesn't go your way this time, it doesn't define you as a person or change your self-worth. There is always another path that's more right for you. If your goals are making you anxious, it may be time to surrender to presence instead.

Passion: This is as simple (and at times as challenging) as leading with your heart in everything you do and share. Allow whatever is lighting you up from the inside to radiate out of you. Passion is 'pathos', the language of the heart, and being heart-driven requires us to share our 'heart story', arguably the most impactful tool we have. This is what moves us, moves people and ultimately moves mountains.

Energetically, the heart is the most powerful organ in the body. Its frequency can be measured seven metres away. Who knows how far the ripples of the heart can travel if we explore and share our lives passionately?

Play: Now, this doesn't necessarily mean we have to go old school by hitting up the swings and slides, although that's actually bloody fun and highly recommended (your inner child will love you, just don't push the little kids off the swings). Rather, it's about finding ways to make life light and to gamify things. It's to adventure, to experiment, to remain curious, and to explore the infinite depths of our imagination. Play is crucial to our sense of joy. It helps to laugh, self-deprecate and not take things too seriously or get caught in life's infinite melodramas. It also means bringing a mindset of celebration to everything you do. It's so easy to get bogged down or to be our own biggest critic, but celebrating reminds us that what we do and create is wonderful, and we should always be our biggest champions!

I believe that play gets trained out of us in the process of becoming 'responsible' working adults and that when we aren't playful, we often slide into fear. Play also enables us to access our innate capacity for problem-solving, creativity and intuition. Not to mention it's just plain fun.

When I owned my fitness studio, PITFIT, one of the first classes I created was called 'Play'. It was an opportunity to gamify fitness with silly things like pool-noodle fights, scarecrow tiggy and team-based activities that earned points. The desired outcome of the class was to build cardio fitness. Sure, this can happen on a gruelling run around the block or a cycle through the streets, or by being a sadistic bitch and making people do burpees all class, but the heart and lungs don't know or care how they are being tested. For many people, forty-five minutes of games where you're simply having a laugh while you sweat is a far more enjoyable process than grinding it out, pounding the pavement for three-quarters of an hour or vomiting in the gym toilets after burpee 462.

The same goes for my time onstage. When things get too serious for me in stage world, I know I've forgotten about the importance of play. One of the things I've learned to do over the years is incorporate a little game prior to the performance of a long-running show. On my dressing room mirror, I keep Post-it notes, all containing words or phrases to do with the character I'm portraying. During my time playing the Phantom, these would include things like 'danger', 'obsession', 'senses', 'magic' or 'music'. I would close my eyes, turn around three times and hopefully point at the mirror. Whichever Post-it note my finger pointed closest to would be the idea I would play with that performance. This didn't change things drastically, but it did keep me in the here and now, focused and present, and allowed me to bring a sense of play to the show that always made it more fun. It also gave my scene partners something they could use to throw something new back at me and, in the confines of the scene and story, we were just passing that ball back and forth. It helped keep everything feeling fresh.

Persistence: It's important to know that life isn't an exact science. We can observe all the previous five power P's, but sometimes things still won't go our way. That's fine though – we controlled what we could control, and we sustained our power and had agency, but we need number six: persistence. Life is sometimes about taking the knocks and getting back up. It's also about objectively reflecting.

Ask yourself: Are you prepared? Have you put in all the technical work required? Are you being present and exploring the process rather than focusing on outcomes? What's your why? Do you feel passionate about what you're exploring, or do you need to get curious? Where might you be able to add more play to your life? Are you celebrating yourself? If you fall off, are you getting back up on the horse?

These six simple steps enable us to acknowledge and discern what we can control and what we can't – an invaluable component of expanding our sense of awareness.

Expecting, accepting and controlling

Expectations play a huge part in our experience of life. We often want to fix, change and control. We become disappointed or frustrated when someone, like a partner, friend, or colleague, doesn't meet our expectations or projections. The same goes for situations – how often do you do something with an expectation of how it should go, then become angry, frustrated or disappointed if it doesn't go the way you thought it would? We repeat this habit over and over rather than accepting that we only play a part in what happens, that we can only control so much and that people and situations are exactly as they are, not how we would like them to be. Nobody expects a tree or an ocean to do something different. No-one expects the sun to do anything other than rise in the east. We simply accept it as it is. How different would the world be if we treated ourselves and others with that same level of acceptance?

I spent much of my time working with Ben Crowe discussing the things that are in my control as a performer (and as a human being) and the things that are out of my control. When it comes to the stage, there have been many times when I've been caught in the trap of trying to control things I couldn't to get a desired outcome: things like sound quality, the way another actor delivers their line or how the orchestra is playing that phrase of music. This is common for a lot of people. We tend to want to control things because we're afraid of how they might look if we relinquish control and surrender to the moment. However, we can't control everything. The outcome of any situation is always a combination of the things we can control and the things we can't, and we need to learn to accept that.

When there is someone special in the audience – a friend I want to impress, my family, the creative team, the producers, a particular reviewer – I want it all to go perfectly. It rarely does. There are countless other things that are inherently out of my control in a live theatre setting. It might be a set piece failing, a lighting cue not working, the conductor missing a cue, a speaker breaking, or a bunch of 'Just Stop Oil' protestors jumping onstage mid-performance of *Les Misérables* to proclaim that their plight is like Jean Valjean's plight, then handcuffing themselves to the set for the best part of an hour before having the show cancelled and later getting arrested. Yes, I was actually onstage that night (face-palm emoji)!

The simple fact is that sometimes things go wrong, and the best thing you can do is acknowledge that fact and accept it into your life. I could bore you with infinite serious stories, but let's have some fun.

Over the years, I've endured a fair few costume malfunctions onstage. Shoes breaking, hems splitting, cloaks getting stuck in set pieces, the list goes on. But from the moment I stepped onto the stage, the specific malfunction that's haunted me most is none other than the dreaded crotch curse. This is when, for some unknown reason, the theatre gods take pleasure in ensuring your pants split right where your junk is.

I was first struck with the crotch curse in my final year of high school while playing Judas in *Jesus Christ Superstar*. You would think a pair of skintight leather bike pants could withstand a run of six shows ... alas, it wasn't to be. On my final performance, the zip split, and my pants started falling down. Rather than just accepting what was clearly out of my control, I spent most of the number, front and centre with my arse to the audience, singing with a mic in one hand while using the other hand to try to fix the unfixable. I exited the stage crestfallen with embarrassment.

The second major one occurred while playing the Phantom in London. There's a moment with about fifteen minutes to go in the show when the Phantom decides it's all or nothing and gets down on one knee to propose to his magnificent infatuation, Christine. One night, as my knee hit the ground, I felt a huge rip. Luckily, the Phantom is wearing a cloak at that point, so whatever damage had occurred was concealed from the audience. I ran offstage at the end of that scene and let my dresser know what tragedy had ensued.

My dresser and I had a quick look at the damage under the cloak. Shit! It was a nuts-to-knee split, and the final scene that went for about ten minutes and had no cloak was coming up shortly. We were going to have to make some serious adjustments on the fly after the next scene (thankfully also cloaked) if I was going to get through the final one without challenging the blokes down the road in *Magic Mike*. As I punted my gondola through a lake of candelabras and back onto the stage, my voice was singing but my mind was conjuring up my dresser's options (control freak!). I figured she had three. One, quickly run upstairs and grab another pair of pants. No, that won't work, not enough time. Two, grab half-a-dozen or so safety pins and calmly go about the meticulous job of threading and pinning her way down my leg. Way too precarious. Final option, the stapler ... that'll hold it.

As I ran offstage and took my cloak off, assuming she'd read my mind, I waited for her to bring out the stapler, but there was no stapler to be seen. Nope, she'd gone for the safety pins. In the ninety seconds she had, nervous and fumbling, she threaded and pinned a big fat zero. Fuck! I felt so bad for her and didn't want her to get in any strife, so I thought, 'Okay, it's up to me now. I have to manage these ten minutes without the audience seeing my undies.' Once again, I went for the high-school option and turned my back to the audience wherever possible, or I bevelled (dance terminology for a sort of effeminate thigh-on-thigh pose), trying to cover up my flesh and undies from the audience while hanging on to what I can of the character's integrity and hopefully not looking like an old showgirl.

After the performance, I washed my make-up off, got changed and went to leave when I spotted my director outside the stage door. Oh no ... of all the nights he happened to be watching, it had to be this one. I turned to make a quick escape, but we locked eyes, so I approached him sheepishly. 'Did you enjoy the show?' I asked innocently. He responded quickly and abrasively: 'What the hell were you doing in the final scene? You looked like a washed-up old showgirl out there.'

Face-palm!

The final curse took place while playing Jean Valjean on the West End. At the top of the show, the character has a heartbreaking, epic soliloquy where he sheds all his anger, shame and pain. There's an iconic moment where he falls to his knees, front and centre, as he screams out, 'This is all I have lived for, this is all I have knowwwwwn!' Once again, riiiip! The middle seam of my pants went and, this time, I finally decided to accept that I have no control over the crotch curse, no control over who sees my undies or my junk, if anything flops out. It was just me, a few high B flats, a thousand-plus people and a tight pair of black spandex Bonds.

Boy, was it one of the most freeing onstage feelings. I'm pretty sure I slid my knees out a little further just in case anyone decided to take a snap. There was a real sense of joy and release in accepting the situation and surrendering to that moment, allowing everything out of my control to just happen and gifting the first few rows with a bit more than their money's worth. It was a great reminder for me to 'control the controllables', and I was glad I was tested with the curse one more time. It felt like the theatre gods were asking me if I had learned anything, and I think it's safe to say I had a good old chuckle with them. We have to laugh at ourselves – it's far more fun that way!

So much of life is out of our control that the question isn't whether things are going to happen or not – they're always going to happen, and we need to expect that. Rather, the question is: How do we respond to those things? Do we try to cover them up or resist them, judge them, or get angry or frustrated by them? Or do we accept them as they are and, with grace, allow them to run their course, adding to the unique, quirky tapestry of our lives? Maybe we even find an opportunity to giggle along the way, both with them and at ourselves.

The sounds of silence

Another important part of cultivating presence is actively listening. Listening is one of the most ancient forms of meditation. It's shamanic in many ways. When I'm not present or I'm focusing too heavily on the future, I'm generally not listening, or certainly not listening well, to either the external world or my internal world. That little voice of wisdom and deep knowing gets drowned out by all the surface noise. Listening actively brings us back to the present moment. The quieter we are, the easier it is for us to hear, and that doesn't just apply to the outside world.

Exercise: active listening

Listen to the sounds around you. You can do this with your eyes open or closed – I prefer to do it with them open for a more physically grounded experience.

Notice all the sounds around you without thinking about them. Just notice them. Maybe it's the sound of the traffic, the sound of the birds, the sound of the wind or rain, the sound of people talking or walking nearby, the sound of your breath, hopefully not the sound of tinnitus. Notice the full soundscape as one large entity.

Now, begin to shift your awareness between sounds within the soundscape. Spend a few moments on one sound, then the next, then the next. There may be a new sound that comes into your soundscape – notice that one too.

Shift your awareness to the farthest sound from you. Notice it for a few moments, then shift your awareness to the sound closest to you. Do this without judgement or storylines – just notice them.

Now bring your awareness back to the full soundscape for a few moments and enjoy the feeling of being immersed and a part of it. Bring that awareness internally, focusing on your breath, and listen out for that little voice, the wise, knowing one within you. You might call it your intuition, or you might call it something else. Sit and listen, can you hear it?

After a few moments of immersion, however long you choose, gently let go of your awareness of the internal and external sounds and go about your day with this new-found presence and, maybe, some new-found wisdom.

You can do this exercise as often as you like throughout the day. I love it side-stage before going on as it really helps me cultivate more presence. It gets me out of my thinking mind and into my deeper, intuitive self, the other actors, and the sonic detail of the world around me.

Abundance: there's enough to go around

Another way to step outside of fear is through a very simple mindset shift from scarcity to abundance. Abundance mindset is basically the idea that there are enough resources and opportunities in the world for me and everyone else. Scarcity is the opposite of that, the thought that if someone receives something then I won't receive it or I have less chance of receiving it. Where scarcity mindset has a cap on possibilities, abundance mindset says possibilities are infinite.

In the competitive world of showbiz, scarcity mindset is rife. From audition rooms to casting announcements, to private conversations to opening night performances, there's always a group of people who feel like someone else's success is their loss. If I had a dollar for the number of complaints I've heard over the years that come from a scarcity mindset, I'd be investing in musicals rather than performing in them. I've learned over time to energetically disconnect from those kinds of people as that negativity is not something I need in my life.

I once worked with an extraordinarily talented artist whose scarcity mindset was an internal prison for them. They were constantly complaining about something. They rarely expressed joy for what they were doing, but their self-worth was totally defined by what they were doing ... See where this is going? There was always someone they were comparing themselves to, someone more attractive and more talented with a better job and more followers on social media. I had an amicable working friendship with this person – they would share their discontent with me and often seek some philosophical or spiritual advice or the right book to help them see their plight from another angle. There was a warmth to the friendship. I understood them.

One day, we came into work and were notified by our creative team that the producers would be coming to see the show later that week. Suddenly, this person's mood changed towards me. They were cold and hostile, refusing to engage with me in scenes, rarely making eye contact and no longer chatting to me offstage. This happened for a couple of shows. During that time, I racked my brain to think of what I possibly could have done. I hadn't spoken about them unkindly behind their back, nothing had happened onstage and I had barely chatted to them offstage. Accepting that I may have missed something, at the end of the next show I pulled them aside to ask them what was upsetting them and if there was anything I had done to hurt them. They were adamant I hadn't done anything, but their behaviour didn't reflect that.

Deciding to call them out on it (or call them in, as Rob Mills discusses on season two of the BTM podcast), I said, 'Well, you've been incredibly cold and avoiding me for the past day or so. Either something's up, which you're welcome to share or not share without judgement, or I've done something to upset you, in which case I'd like to know so I can apologise.' After a moment of thought, they turned to me and said, 'Well, the producers are coming to see the show. They're just gonna watch your stuff and leave and not even see my stuff.' I was baffled. 'Really?' I replied, 'that's what's been troubling you? Firstly, I'm positive they'll stay for the whole show – that's their job – and they'll love what you're sharing out there. Secondly, and probably more importantly, if they do leave early, that's *not my* fault, and you have no right to blame that on me or be cold towards me because of it.'

Their response to being called out (or in) was immediate regret, shame and an apology. I didn't take it personally, as I knew it wasn't really about me, but I'm glad I had the wherewithal to stand up to them and point out the glaringly obvious. This had everything to do with their scarcity mindset, their limiting beliefs and the false notion that there wasn't room for multiple people to be seen, heard and appreciated. It was their suffering. They felt that if I was acknowledged, they somehow wouldn't or couldn't be.

Conversely, I have another friend in showbiz – let's call him Robert. I admire Robert to no end. He has one of those infectious personalities. Everyone is always better for time spent with him. Robert is never bogged down in one thing for too long; he has a varied career that allows him to constantly be creatively challenged. He doesn't fear change; instead, he is malleable and sees change as an opportunity for something new and exciting. When there isn't work coming directly to Robert, he loves to create work, not just for himself but for many others as well. Robert stays on his path, sometimes quietly, sometimes screaming joyously and proudly from the rooftops, but always with immense appreciation for what he has, rather than what he doesn't have. He never feels like someone else's journey should be his journey, and he's not fazed by others having success. In fact, he generously celebrates the success of others. He believes wholeheartedly in being the rising tide to lift all boats. Sure, he's not immune to struggles and strife, but it's how he responds to those moments that made him special. Robert knows that there's room enough for everyone. We all need a Robert in our life.

Scarcity is a derivative of fear and although it is common for artists or those who work in a gig economy, it's not exclusive to them. It's anyone who is constantly questioning where the next gig, the next pay cheque, pay rise, promotion or shot of validation is coming from. Fundamentally, it's an ability to be comfortable and confident in the present moment, and this only adds to unnecessary anxiety and stress. We must have the awareness and the courage to simultaneously aspire to goals and dreams, and trust that we're okay in the here and now. Ultimately choosing derivatives of love always serves us better than choosing derivatives of fear.

Journal exercise: honest reflections

This is a great time to reflect upon your current mindset. Are you operating from scarcity or abundance? Do you have limiting self-beliefs, or are your possibilities limitless? Are you charitable and loving in your ways? Are you helping, celebrating and lifting others up, or does someone else's success invalidate you? Are you fixated on things being the way they are, or are you open to change and going with the flow of life?

We can all work on our abundance mindset through certain areas in our life that feel more abundant than others. A great way to shift more towards abundance is by acknowledging what we do have rather than what we don't. Enter ...

Gratitude

Gratitude is our ability to appreciate and give thanks for the things we have in our lives. In this way, gratitude and abundance are closely linked. They are both connected to internally valuing what is already in our lives, rather than needing something more to come in or for someone else to have less, for us to feel satisfied, full or enough.

Gratitude doesn't just randomly make us feel great ... there's plenty of science to it as well. It is known to regulate cortisol in the brain and reduce anxiety and stress. It increases our happy hormones (dopamine and serotonin) by focusing on the wonderful things we have in our life rather than the things we are lacking. Research suggests that we can shift into a gratitude mindset in as little as three weeks, but it requires conscious action.

We might think that we're practising gratitude all the time but, unless it's conscious, unfortunately the happy hormones don't come out to play. Enter gratitude journalling. This is something that has become very popular, so there are countless books you can buy that prompt your daily gratitude practice. These are a great way to facilitate your gratitude journey, but many miss a crucial aspect.

Gratitude is not a thought that you have or a bunch of words you write down. Although words and thoughts do have their place in gratitude, they are missing the critical ingredient – *feeling*! If the body's reaction to gratitude is a spike in happy hormones, we have to actually *feel* grateful to produce that hormonal response. We can't just think grateful thoughts or write a bunch of shit down to say OMG we, like, did our gratitude practice today, snaps to us! This is like buying a home, getting the keys and not living in it. A gratitude home must be lived in – it's not an investment property, people! There will be no negative gearing in Gratitude-ville, thank you very much! To muddy over a gratitude practice and just think, 'Oh yeah, I'm grateful for my dog, I'm grateful for my job and I'm grateful for my family' doesn't cut it. We must spend time with those thoughts, reflect on them and allow the feeling or the feelings they bring up to percolate inside us. You can't rush your gratitude practice. Like all great practices, it takes time, patience, diligence and dedication, but it can be life-changing.

It goes without saying that I feel immense gratitude for the countless opportunities and experiences I've had along my journey as a performer, but I didn't bring conscious awareness to gratitude until five or so years ago when I took up journalling religiously. Since then, I've seen my mindset shift astronomically. Things that I used to complain about that weighed me down or negative ideas I would cycle through that led me to scarcity conversations and thought patterns now rarely arise and, when they do, I can check myself. They are instead replaced with far more grounded, contented thoughts and a deep appreciation for what I *do* have. I often feel such an overwhelming sense of gratitude that it radiates throughout my body, and I quite literally feel warm tingles down to my toes. This is awareness and bliss manifested into physical sensation, and it's incredible.

Here is the simple gratitude journalling exercise I learned some years ago that I do each morning. Give it a go, and see how radically your mindset changes both in terms of your happy hormones and your ability to see the world from a place of abundance.

Journal exercise: gratitude

Have your journal handy. Sit down with your eyes closed or lightly open and begin to think of three things. They can be a person, a pet, a place, an event, an experience, an opportunity or even a part of yourself that you are grateful for.

Now, the important part. Cast your mind's eye on those things. Let's say it's your pet that you're grateful for. Visualise them in their best ways. Look into their eyes and notice all the feelings that come up for you. Lean into them and allow them all to wash over you and fill you up from the inside out. Is it love, joy, laughter or awe? Maybe you feel a warmth or a tingling sensation in your body. Note it all. It shouldn't take more than a few moments on each to be overcome with gratitude. Once you're feeling full, open your eyes then write down the things you're grateful for and how they made you feel.

Repeat this exercise daily, preferably first thing in the morning or before bed. The things you're grateful for might change or might stay the same. You could be grateful for the sound of your partner's farts – it doesn't matter. What you're grateful for is far less important than the experience and the feeling of being grateful.

As you practise this exercise over the coming days, weeks and months, be aware of your mindset and behavioural shifts and write them down too. This is powerful stuff that affects your neural pathways and changes your habitual patterns. If you have consciously done this work, then you are entering a profound process of mental rewiring. Writing down how your mindset is changing will keep you motivated to continue.

Breathe and take your time

Close to twenty years ago, I completed a Bachelor of Arts majoring in Musical Theatre at what is now Federation University in Ballarat, Victoria. During my three years of study, we took part in an array of subjects that all pertained to the craft and skills needed to perform in musicals. No, 'jazz hands' is not a subject! It did, however, include singing technique, acting, acting through song, tap, jazz and ballet dancing, theatre history and music studies. But, on reflection, the class that taught me the most was voice class: not singing voice, just 'the voice' (John Farnham was also sadly not a subject at uni).

Voice class was run by an older chap by the name of Stephen Costan. Stephen was your typical, regal Shakespearean-actor type. He was heavyset and had a pointed, well-groomed whitish-grey beard. He sat in his chair and his effortlessly booming voice reverberated around the room, giving the impression that his career as an actor was generally best spent on a throne playing King Lear, King Richard or some other kind of king.

Stephen had us perform an array of seemingly peculiar exercises: rolling around the room and cartwheeling into walls while singing or staring into space while whispering sounds like 'kor' and 'ki' in patterns of seven as we inhaled and exhaled. I'm pretty sure that if you locked eyes with him, he would give you some flirty eyes back. In fact, he once said, 'I can be flirty,' which had us all in stitches. He also once tried to teach us to breathe into one lung. I immediately called my father, a doctor, to get a medical professional's opinion on whether this was indeed humanly possible. Turns out it's not, and I, being a know-it-all little brat, took great pleasure in informing Stephen of this fact. Turns out he knew that too and was referring to an ability to isolate the ribcage and the muscles on one side of the body while you breathe, which is actually pretty impressive. (I know ... you're trying it now!) Serves me right for being bratty.

However, there was one activity that I'll never forget – I've thought about it many times over the past twenty years. We were asked to prepare a monologue of no more than one page. One by one, we would stand up before Stephen and the class to share it. When my turn came around, I stood in position a few metres away from Stephen on his chair (throne) while my classmates sat cross-legged around him. 'Now is the winter of our discontent,' I said in a contrived Shakespearean tone. 'Slower,' replied Stephen. 'Breathe and take your time.' So, I said it slower. Again, Stephen chimed in, 'Slower. Breathe and take your time!' This went on and on until he finally asked me to sit down and join the confused mob.

Some weeks later, as this practice went on, I finally got what Stephen was asking of us. He wanted us to find comfort in discomfort, to be vulnerable, to be patient (one of the most important virtues for any performer), to be able to hold a space and draw an audience in without uttering a word. He was teaching us that acting doesn't just rely on speaking – it's in the thought processes between the words, the gravitas of stillness and, of course, the wonder of the breath. He was teaching us that, through breath, we could calm our nervous systems in the face of adversity and nervous energy and reclaim our onstage power.

I've been to many breath workshops and classes over the years, devoting energy and attention to different styles of breathing, but the first person to help me understand the true power of the breath and its importance in everything, including performance, presentations, confronting conversations and many other parts of life, was Stephen Costan. I'm forever thankful and grateful for his lessons.

Exercise: box breathing

This is an exercise Stephen gave us on day one of first-year uni. I now see it practised in breath and yoga studios, fitness classes and by meditators, athletes, psychologists and performers all around the world. It is one of the simplest ways to bring the nervous system out of its anxiety and fear state (the five F's) and back to presence.

You can do this in a chair or with your legs crossed on the floor (feel free to sit on a pillow or a yoga block to elevate your hips if you can't keep an upright posture easily) – you can even do it lying down, whatever is most comfortable for you. Place both hands on your belly. When you're ready, gently close your eyes. Allow the breath to fill up your hands as you naturally breathe into your diaphragm. Breathe in for a steady count of four, and out for a steady count of four. Repeat this a few times.

Now to advance the process. Again, breathe in for four counts, hold the breath at the top of the inhalation for four, then breathe out for four and hold the breath after you exhale for four counts. Repeat this for ten rounds, keeping your focus on the breath. You are now 'box breathing'.

After you've completed your ten rounds, stop focusing on your breath, move your hands away from your diaphragm and spend a few moments noticing how you feel. Is it more rested, more relaxed, calmer?

Note that this is just one* ***very* *simple breathing exercise for bringing the nervous system into the parasympathetic state (the 'calming down' or 'rest and digest' state). There are countless others that promote a different response within the body and I implore you to explore these if it sparks your interest.*

Breath is one of only a few functions of the body that is both autonomic (functions by itself) and somatic (responds to our conscious attention on it). We take this for granted, as breath is our most powerful tool for naturally shifting our physical, chemical and mental states.

Over the past decade, we've seen breath practices become more mainstream as Western science catches up with what Eastern practitioners have spent millennia mastering. In the yogic world, breath exercises are called pranayama. Pranayama can take many forms, all of which rapidly move the energy within us and change our body chemistry. This includes producing more serotonin and dopamine, and possibly DMT (a tryptamine), regulating the nervous system, helping digestion and brain function, and releasing emotional blockages.

If you want to pursue the powerful benefits of breath work, I suggest finding a local yoga studio to practise pranayama (kundalini yoga, in particular, has a big focus on powerful breath exercises), finding a designated breath/meditation studio or engaging in things like tai chi and qigong. Here in Melbourne, I enjoy the classes at The Breath Haus in Richmond. If I can't get to a class, I use their app. I've developed a beautiful friendship with the owners Nathan Freeman and Ella Pike, who feature on season one of the BTM podcast, and I've had some of the most profound and life-changing experiences in their classes.

Somatic healing

One such experience happened before returning to singing in 2024 after almost a year off. I was really stressing out about my return. My voice still hadn't come back properly, and it was the day before my first gig. Yes, the operations were a success, but the stress of it all had started a spiralling bout of reflux, which I suffer with when I'm highly stressed.

Reflux is a nightmare for singers, especially silent reflux (laryngopharyngeal reflux). It's something we don't feel or notice until it fries and inflames the vocal cords, often overnight. I tried to manage it by taking medication, but it was barely working. I could feel my stomach churning, and it was going to take more than a dose of esomeprazole and some Gaviscon to fix it. I could feel it festering.

So, I decided to go to breath class for some somatic therapy. Within a few minutes of lying down, blanket over my body, head on a cushy pillow and with some mindful slow, deep box breathing, I was in the parasympathetic state. But, as the intensity of the breathing started to increase, my body began to convulse, beginning at my solar plexus. This wasn't new to me, it's what's known as a somatic release, and has much to do with the functionality of the vagus nerve (a large nerve that connects the brain and the gut that can affect bowel function, cause throat issues and increase brain fog and your heart rate). The convulsing became wild, totally out of control, and I just allowed it to pass through me.

I began to feel like my body was levitating, but my hands felt like they had rocks attached to them. It was like my higher self was leaving my body in some way. I even began speaking in whispering tongues, repeating the phrase 'you are one, you are one, you are one'. Oneness is something I believe in deeply – the oneness of humanity, the oneness of the soul, the oneness of love – my meditation teaching certification is even through the organisation 1 Giant Mind, and I will discuss more of this later in the book.

None of this felt that strange to me. I allowed it all to happen without judging it. When I woke up the next morning, I felt lighter, like whatever was churning, whatever I had been carrying, had left. What's more, my voice felt freer than it had in a year and the gig went off without a hitch.

Don't beat yourself up

An important part of all this self-learning and self-discovery is that we are constantly in flux between learning, forgetting and remembering, or the other way around. For weeks on end, we will feel like we are taking consistent leaps forward as we put some of these great meditation, mindset, spiritual and philosophical practices into place. It's a wonderful feeling, like we can finally use these ingredients to cook up a well-balanced mental and emotional health meal each day. But then something unexpected comes into our lives, the universe challenges us again and it knocks us off our course, or we are bogged down with work and family life, the rat-race of the capitalist world we live in. We lose that rhythm and begin to forget our practices.

What's important is to truly love ourselves despite the merry-go-round of learning, forgetting and remembering. Give yourself the grace to get it wrong sometimes, to be imperfect, to fall off the horse and get back on. Sure, we all want to stay disciplined, but it's equally valuable to have ease and softness and to not beat ourselves up for not getting it right all the time. Remember that the expectation that we are perfect may be one that other people place on us, but it doesn't need to be one that we place on ourselves. Also, self-loathing is just our fear state manifesting. We don't want to live there anymore.

When we take off our masks, vulnerably accepting our imperfections, embracing both discomfort and an abundance mindset while consciously expanding our self-awareness, we have the opportunity and capacity to reclaim this natural state then find our bliss.

4

PART 4

Bliss

Recognising the presence of bliss

By shifting our relationship with fear and expanding our sense of awareness, we can begin to experience a state of *bliss* more frequently. Before you get any ideas, I'm not suggesting you mung out on extreme doses of acid and watch on as your pet dog morphs into a rainbow-coloured unicorn. Bliss is the English translation of the Sanskrit word *ananda*. Ironically, ananda is so ineffable that it cannot be described, but the closest English definition is bliss. You may have heard of anandamide, which is one of the body's natural forms of cannabinoids. It is often referred to as the 'bliss neurotransmitter' and is similar to THC, which prompts feelings of relaxation, happiness and ... bliss.

Bliss is used in English to describe a feeling of euphoria, but bliss as a state isn't about being permanently euphoric. It's the state in which our mind, heart and body have a feeling of safety, security, calm, connection, freedom and, most importantly, presence. It's not about trying to be permanently high or happy – happiness is just another emotion that passes through us.

As an aside, society should probably place a lot less emphasis on trying to be happy all the time and more energy on trying to sustain bliss. Bliss feels incredibly grounded – it's solid, like the roots of a beautiful old willow, a place that isn't trapped in thoughts, anxieties, worries, stresses, traumas or fears.

I'd argue that what we're truly after in life is not just those successes or achievements – the fancy watch, the bigger house or the better lifestyle – but the *feeling* we envisage we are going to receive from those experiences and possessions. That feeling is bliss. We all know this feeling, so how can we actively choose to feel sustained bliss more often, without relying purely on those extrinsic things?

Fortunately, that's very simple. We experience it when met with the ceaseless beauty of nature, when enthralled in a book, while listening to our favourite music, when at the theatre, when we sing freely and dance wildly, while having intimate and passionate sex or when engaging in deep chats and big belly laughs. We experience it when we're travelling to new places or simply gazing lovingly into the eyes (soul) of another. Most importantly, we meet it when we find the spark inside of us, that truly lights us up. *Our bliss!*

When did you last make the time to take in a sunrise

or sunset on the beach, to go see that band you love bust out their bangers, to play the role of tourist with child-like eyes, or just stop to fully take in that someone special? In all these moments, there is no fear, anxiety or stress – there is simply the here and now, the majesty and simplicity of the present moment. In that presence, we experience bliss. And, although we think it's elusive, something attained purely from our experiences in the world, bliss doesn't rely on any of these moments – the common denominator in all these experiences is *us*, which is exactly where bliss resides. We don't have to look very far to experience it – we have the capacity to access it whenever we like, wherever we like, from within. Presence is our gateway to bliss.

So, how do we bring our bliss to life? Well, it's not abiding by 'should's' – pleasing others and society in ways that render us living a life half-lived. The true answer lies in the innate wisdom and courage of our hearts.

There is a Sanskrit mantra: *sat-chit-ananda* – existence, consciousness, bliss. For me, that evokes the idea that we must spend time going inward, delving into our deeper consciousness. Meditating into the heart, we are not only met with the burning fire of our bliss, but begin to see what's getting in the way of us following it. It's rarely a comfortable journey to embark on. The famous Chinese proverb, that a lotus flower is born out of the mud, speaks to this. There may be much mud to trudge through – and some blisters – but this is the work! Washing off the muck of conditioning, appeasment and self-limitation that's concealing our bliss, and transcending that critical voice which ruthlessly repeats, 'you couldn't possibly!' But, as American literature professor Joseph Campbell once said, 'If you follow your bliss, you put yourself on a kind of track that has been there all the while waiting for you.'

Meditation

For me, there is no better way to find presence or to expand my sense of awareness than to meditate. It is the most powerful tool to get back to being present and simply being. Earlier on, during my rant about bums, I mentioned that meditation also helps us expand our ability to be discerning – to pick and choose which trains of thought we follow. There are many other benefits to meditation: reduced stress and anxiety, increased empathy, increased focus, a boosted immune system and improved sleep.

Sadly, there are also a lot of misconceptions and myths that stop people doing it. As a qualified meditation teacher, I've heard them all – it's too hard, it's too spiritual or religious, I can't sit with my legs crossed, I meditate while I'm running (I'm pretty sure you run while you're running), and I don't have enough time in the day. Well, as the Zen saying goes, 'You should sit in meditation for twenty minutes a day. Unless you're too busy, then you should sit for an hour.'

But the most common misconception I hear from people is that they just can't stop their thoughts, so there's no point in meditating. Fact: neither can I! Nor can pretty much anybody in the world unless you're a monk meditating in a temple for eighteen hours a day. Even then, I would question how quickly those thoughts would come rushing back when faced with the hectic sensory overload of places like Shibuya in Tokyo, Piccadilly Circus in London or Times Square in New York City.

In short, we are hardwired to think. But, thankfully, we are not our thoughts (I think we would probably all be in jail if we actually were, I certainly would be!), we are the awareness of that thought, as discussed in the previous chapter. René Descartes' *cogito, ergo sum* – I think, therefore I am – expresses so poetically that he was simply the awareness witnessing his thinking. 'Thinking' is the *action*, 'I am' is the *awareness*, the *atman*, that chooses the action. We are also not our physical bodies. Nobody says 'I am leg' or 'I am hand'. It's 'my leg', 'my hand' – who is the 'my'? The awareness.

Meditation can be very simply defined as the practice of expanding our self-awareness. I also like to think of it as a pathway back to our deepest self, to soul. It's not about stopping thoughts at all, but changing our relationship with them.

Make 'discernment' your middle name

Think about it: our thoughts become our words, words become actions, actions become habits, and those habits affect us and everyone and everything we encounter. When we clue into that idea, we see how responsible we are for our thoughts and how powerful they can be. Meditation offers us the opportunity to create space between our true self and our thoughts and therefore the ability to see our thoughts played out in front of us. We can then choose which ones we would like to follow and which ones we don't want or need to. This is the definition of discernment.

Discernment is a wonderful thing – it cultivates rational choices and positive thinking. It helps us to not take things personally, to react less emotionally, to control what we can, to be less judgemental, and to pick our battles. The challenging thing about discernment is that it's kind of like clothes – if we don't wash them, over time they get dirty and smelly. The same goes for discernment. We have to consistently bathe in awareness to keep up our ability to discern, and the simplest way to wash ourselves in awareness is to meditate.

Exercise: discernment cultivation meditation

Try this simple meditation, which I often practise before going onstage. This takes about three minutes, but you're welcome to enjoy it for longer.

Find a comfortable seat – you don't need to have your legs crossed with your fingers and thumbs together guru-style. Any seated position that makes you feel comfy is perfect, just ensure your back is upright, your head and neck aren't resting on anything (it may cause you to become sleepy, and it's best to stay awake when we meditate!) and that your palms are gently resting in your lap or on your knees.

When you're ready, close your eyes. As you do so, notice how you're feeling. You might be feeling anxious, energised, a little stressed or something else. Without any judgement, just sit with those feelings and notice them.

Now, starting at the top of your head, very slowly begin to scan down your body, noticing every intricate physical detail. The forehead, the eyes, the nose, jaw, neck, shoulders, chest, arms, hands and so on ... all the way down to your toes.

Now, send your awareness to three physical sensations you're feeling: it could be the sensation of your feet on the floor, your clothes brushing against your skin, your hands resting in your lap or maybe some other sensation. Once again, no labels or judgements, just notice them.

Finally, move your awareness to your breath. Notice the movement of the next three breaths: how the belly and ribs expand, how the chest and shoulders rise or maybe the light breeze in and out of your nose as you inhale and exhale. Continue a soft, focused awareness of your breath.

As your mind wanders, which it will – it's totally normal and an integral part of the meditation – just ever so gently bring it back to the breath. Stick with this for as long as you like, whether that's three or twenty minutes – that's up to you. When you're ready, slowly shift your awareness away from your breath, take a few moments to really notice how you're feeling and how that may have shifted from when you first closed your eyes, then gently blink your eyes open and calmly continue on with your day.

Remember, discernment gives us incredible agency in life. When we have that space between who we truly are (the awareness) and the thoughts bubbling away in our mind, we suddenly see that we have choice in every moment. We have a choice of what to think, what to say, what to do and how to act. Life is a series of fork-in-the-road moments: in every part of every day, we can choose between multiple avenues. If the average person has approximately 60,000 thoughts a day, ask yourself this: Are you choosing your thoughts calmly and consciously with gentle awareness? Are you able to respond (or be response-able) to each one as it arises, or are your thoughts the master and you a puppet mindlessly reacting to them? If your answer is the latter, remind yourself that if we aren't training our self-awareness, then we are putting ourselves in countless situations that are mindless, regrettable and detrimental. Meditation gives us the opportunity to show up as our most calm, resilient, grounded, discerning and aware self. I don't know about you, but that's when I make my best choices.

Finding the divine in the daily

When it comes to the idea of sustaining bliss, I know what you're thinking. What about the relentless daily grind of parenting or my mundane job, with my close-talking halitosis-ridden boss who always insists on meeting in person? I hear you, and yes, family life, work life and bosses with bad breath aren't always blissful in the moment, I get that. They can be an absolute pain in the arse. But the moment immediately after our grievance can be blissful, and this is where it's simplest and easiest to comprehend the intrinsic relationship bliss has with an awareness of the present moment.

How many wonderful moments and experiences do you think you've missed out on because you've decided to re-engage with a negative moment over and over again and complain about it? Remember the path of the second suffering? By definition, complaining isn't blissful. Of course, there may be a major crisis or tragic moment in your life that you need to sit in and grieve, or to express in order to process and heal, and this is normal and healthy. But most of our complaining is wasted energy, robbing us of bliss.

We see this with work life all the time. When we start a new job, there is a freshness and an excitement for something new – we are learning every moment. In that learning, we find presence and, in that presence, we find bliss. But, over the course of time, as work becomes predictable and mundane, complaints start dominating our discussions and pressure, stress or issues with colleagues get to us. The state of bliss wanes. Sure, it's natural to have days when we don't feel like fronting up, when there are complications or conflicts, or maybe days when work is a little boring, frustrating or tedious. But remember that bliss is a state, expressed fully in the present moment, so repetitive and mundane can also be blissful if we find ways to sustain our presence in it, bring some play to it or simply remain curious. Side note: offering your boss an Eclipse or Fisherman's Friend may not always encapsulate presence, but it *is* always a present ... try it!

The power of curiosity

As a singer and actor who's made a living out of performing in shows eight times a week, I'm certainly no stranger to repetition or monotony. The interview question I get asked more than any other is: How do you do the same thing show after show after show?

My answer is simple: 'It's not the same, and it's never the same.' It might be the same dots and words on the page, with the same costumes and staging and the same actors but, as no person ever feels the same on any given day, no moment onstage can ever be the same. Most people think that we work hard in the lead-up to opening night, but that's only part of it – the really interesting work starts *after* opening night. That's when, as artists, we get the opportunity to be even more curious, to go in and find more detail, texture, layers and nuance to the roles we play.

Being curious as often as possible has helped me become an artist I'm proud of, one who's constantly digging for greater depth and nuance to my performances. Do I find it every time? Absolutely not. But bringing curiosity to my work is one of a few ways I've learned to keep me present and in process mode throughout the run of a show. So while curiosity doesn't make each and every performance new, it makes every performance richer. There's presence, focus, diligence, connection, reverence, play and love in it, and that makes for much bliss.

This, I might add, is something I've had to learn to lean into and is a far cry from my mindset almost twenty years ago when I started. Back then, curiosity wasn't on my mind at all. There was no more exciting feeling than my agent calling to tell me I had landed a gig. What a mega hit of dopamine from getting such epic levels of validation. Then there's the mega hit of validation from telling my friends and family, the people you love most, giving you the most amount of love in celebration. After that, there was telling the world (my echo chamber) on social media platforms, pinging with dopamine from that again. After I had told everyone, I was met with a rush and excitement on the first day of rehearsals, which would then subside a bit before the thrill and excitement of opening night. It's a roller-coaster of high after high. But, not long after, there was a lull, a disappointment, a realisation that it's just a job, just the day-to-day slog of it. The excitement had gone. Curiosity was my ticket to maintaining bliss.

One of my least favourite things about the world of musical theatre is what happens when bliss wanes in the cast. Same as above, there is excitement through the rehearsal period and opening weeks, but as a cast starts to become familiar with what happens onstage, and the drama of that is no longer exciting for them, the dramas tend to erupt for certain people offstage. Sometimes there are major things that happen that actually need to be dealt with by company managers and producers. But, in my experience, it's mostly just bored, attention-seeking people who create drama to satisfy the suffering of their egos. Most of these occurrences I either block out, don't engage in, find out about weeks later and, most importantly, happily erase from my memory. I wonder how different things would be if people adopted a curious mindset.

The sacred equation

I have an equation I like to use regularly: routine + sacred = ritual. We are told throughout our lives that humans operate best with some sort of structure ... a routine. For the most part, I think that's very true, whether that's the 8.30 a.m. to 3.30 p.m. school day or the 9–5 office week. It might be a morning coffee, exercising before work, meditating mid-afternoon, daily gratitude journalling, no phone and a cuppa before bed, a daily or weekly walk with a group of friends or having a few frothies or a glass of red at the pub on a Friday to release the stress from the work week. Whether it's daily or weekly (or longer), there are certain things we tend to do and keep doing on repeat.

We naturally gravitate towards routines because we feel out of sync without them and because it makes sense with how the world works. We have a certain number of things to do in a day, and a routine lets us know that we can fit them all in. We know where in our day brushing our teeth, making our bed, sitting in traffic jams, paying taxes and picking up the weekly groceries and the kids from school fit in.

But, when we make something sacred, we add what's referred to as the 'non-ordinary world', something beyond the purely physical and psychological realm in which most of Western society lives on a day-to-day basis. I see sacred as comprising three main elements: gratitude, reverence and devotion. Gratitude gives us a greater appreciation for what we currently have. Reverence is the deepest form of respect and honour we can give to something or someone. And devotion offers up the notion of loyalty and love. When these words become consistent actions, they create a deeper level of consciousness to everything we do, and that's integral to us having a relationship with our highest, deepest self. You might even like to call it a relationship with soul. Ritual is soulful.

Actively slowing down in life and bringing a sense of sacred to the most basic tasks is the language of the soul. It's also the simplest and most practical way to turn a routine into a ritual. We could make that walk a little slower and take in everything around us, rather than being on the phone or scrolling though our socials. It might be paying our mortgage with gratitude for the opportunity and the ability to own a home. It might be thanking our bodies for being able to lift that weight or go for that run. Or it might simply be sipping our morning coffee and really tasting every mouthful, and acknowledging the possibility that it might even be our last mouthful, rather than just using it as a kick in the arse to get us through to midday.

When we live life going through the motions, just plodding along in the 'ordinary world' we can feel a bit limited or even out of whack, like there has to be more to life than this. Similarly, if we are on a continuous spiritual junkie bender, living purely esoterically in the abstract and floating from one high to the next chasing the non-ordinary world, we can also feel disconnected. Ritual blends both – it is the embodiment of living at the intersection of both the ordinary and non-ordinary.

On a side note, one of Asher's great quotes from the *Behind The Mask* podcast is the etymology of the word 'weird'. It stems from the ancient Welsh word *wyrdd*, which means to have one foot in each world. How awesome is that, you bunch of epic weirdos!?

Journal exercise: the sacred

Think about your routines. How can you bring a sense of sacredness to them to make them rituals? Is it by adding greater reverence, a more conscious sense of respect and regard to and for your actions? Is it acknowledging them with deeper gratitude and thanks, sitting in the feeling of full appreciation? Or is it exploring the path of the heart and bringing more devotion to even the simplest tasks? It could be as easy as lighting a candle with that cup of tea then sipping on it slowly, consciously appreciating the nature that surrounds you on that run or appreciating all the sentient beings who had a hand in ensuring your dinner is on the table before you start eating.

Start by jotting down the simple routines you have in your life, like coffee in the morning, your daily exercise or making your bed, and see what happens when you add one or more of the three sacred elements to those routines. Give yourself that extra thirty seconds to engage in the sacred. What changes for you? Where do you feel that change in your body? How does the addition of the sacred elements effect your emotional state? Do you feel a stronger, more soulful relationship by making that routine a ritual?

Keep track of how each of these rituals changes you. Once you get a sense of how they affect your overall wellbeing, look for other ways you can introduce a sense of the sacred into your daily life.

When we turn our routines into rituals, we are far more likely to stick with them, as they speak to our souls. Remember the equation: routine + sacred = ritual.

Nature medicine

Sometimes, bliss eludes us. We have loads going on in our lives, which stresses us out, and we shift back into fear and anxiety. It can be a struggle to notice this or divert our internal traffic back into a state of bliss. What we need is a reliable circuit breaker, something that can always offer us bliss. The answer is nature.

Nature is medicine – that walk in the woods, that beautiful sunset, listening to a chorus of birds, swimming in the ocean or hugging your favourite tree has a profound effect on our mental, emotional, physical and spiritual health. The fear, stress, trauma and anxiety we often feel has a lot to do with our inability to be present but by consciously accessing nature, we are immediately diverted back to presence and back to bliss.

Despite society telling us otherwise, we *are* nature. When we reconnect with nature consciously, we are reconnecting with ourselves, our deep selves. When we are met with a sunrise, we don't just see that colourful horizon – we feel it deeply in all its wonder. It wakes us up and *connects* us back to *our* souls with its infinite beauty. We are, after all, spiritual and soulful beings having a human experience. Connection is everything for us. We are hardwired for it, and that doesn't just mean connection to each other but also to every living thing that surrounds us. The term used for this is symbiosis and when we experience it fully, it's impossible not to experience bliss. Remember – bliss isn't outside of you ... it exists *within* you. We just have to be able to switch the channel back to bliss when we feel like we're disconnected. Nature is one of the easiest and most wonderfully unconditional ways to do this.

Something you might like to think about is creating a

sacred spot for yourself, a sort of shrine or blissful home in nature. It should be somewhere you've had a special experience or that means something of significance to you, a place that enables you to consistently switch the channel back to bliss.

Port Fairy on the south-west coast of Victoria is my place. In fact, I've spent a lot of time writing this book there. Port Fairy is a quaint country town about three and a half hours from Melbourne. It's famous for its annual folk festival, but it also holds annual jazz and classical music festivals. It's peaceful and welcoming – everyone who walks past you says 'g'day' or tilts their head and gives you a wink and a click of the tongue. It's brimming with Michelin-starred restaurants and some unique reefs to surf, but there's one particular spot I frequent religiously – it's the south beach, always a bit cold and fresh from the Southern Ocean that finds its way to Antarctica.

The beach is fringed by basalt rocks, formed from an active volcano in nearby Tower Hill some 34,000 years ago. It has left the beach with a 500m by 100–200m (depending on the tide) pool. When I go out to swim, I'm surrounded by these beautiful amber, ash and black basalt rocks creating a buffer for calm waters. As I look around, I see the waves and endless horizon beyond them, the sand dunes brimming with bird life along the beach and the schools of fish swimming frenetically around me. I also love the fact that most mornings, aside from a few locals walking their dogs, it's just me all alone on that beach, definitely the only human foolish enough to swim in the chilly waters. This is bliss. I feel like I'm coalescing with something much bigger than me, something godly. There's a strong sense of symbiosis, connectedness and oneness with nature, and an equally deep respect and reverence for the native lands and waters of the Gunditjmara people who have called this place home for thousands of years. I experience awe and surrender and feel free, powerful, primal, grateful and joyous. I've meditated, had epiphanies and ideas about my relationships and creative pursuits here. I've seen postcard sunsets and watched stars dance in the night sky. I've smiled, prayed, played, laughed and cried in those waters. They always speak deeply to my soul.

It's important to note that you don't need Port Fairy or any sort of idyllic paradise – you just need a patch of nature. A simple tree is always a great option. It's not about the uniqueness of the location but rather about cultivating a relationship with that spot. It needs to be a place you can go back to time and time again to have a deeper conversation with nature, which, of course, is really a deeper conversation with yourself, with your soul. Soul is an incredibly grounding energy, so make sure your time spent in your sacred spot is barefoot. Your skin needs to be touching the earth to feel the benefits of grounding.

Exercise: bliss meditation

Once you have a sacred space, even if you can't physically access it, you can use it to achieve a state of bliss whenever you like simply by meditating on it. It only takes a few minutes, and you can do it multiple times a day.

Find a comfortable seat, somewhere where you're not going to be disturbed. Ensure your head and neck aren't leaning against anything, close your eyes and take a few deep breaths in and out, slowly extending your exhalation each time. When you feel calm and ready, cast your mind's eye to your sacred spot. Build the visual of your sacred place and paint a more detailed picture of it. Notice the details and nuances of it: how it looks, how it smells and any sounds. Are there any physical sensations you can recall, like the feeling of your feet in the grass?

Now, as you build this picture, notice how you feel – is it more calm, more relaxed, more grounded, more connected, more loving? Is it something else? Bring these feelings to your breath. As you breathe in, allow these feelings to expand to every corner of your body. With every breath out, let them radiate around you, building a sort of energetic bubble. Repeat this four or five times.

Once you are bathing in this state of bliss, let go of your awareness with your breath, then sit with these feelings before slowly opening your eyes.

Be sure to write down some of the blissful feelings you felt in reflection. Remember that we have the power to shift our state whenever and wherever we like with a simple three-minute meditation. It's a powerful tool to have in your pocket. Try this multiple times a day and notice how it changes you.

In many ways, bliss is the opposite of fear. Not only is it that spark inside us which makes us feel truly alive, but it's a willingness to sit in a moment without worrying about the past or the future. When we experience and seek bliss, we are choosing peace in the moment and a connection to the bigger world around us. We are reminded that we are never alone – all things are connected in the moment, and all moments are connected to each other. Once we begin following the path of bliss, it leads us on a journey from the inward to the outward. The bliss lighting us up from inside is no longer purely for our own benefit, but a part of something we can share outwardly to have a positive impact on the world and those around us. This is the inherent interplay between bliss and purpose.

5

PART 5

Purpose

The heart of purpose

Now we have taken off our masks, embraced discomfort and stepped into our fears, expanded our sense of awareness and begun to both recognise and follow our bliss, it's time to establish our purpose so that we can share it with the world and serve in positive ways. In the opening chapters of the book, I asked you to write down your core values, your intrinsic self-beliefs, the qualities that make you authentically you. If you've struggled to identify these things, ask a few close friends and family members – people who have known you incredibly well for an exceptionally long period of time. See which answers overlap and which ones resonate with you. I believe we have to know our core values as well as what we stand for, our non-negotiables, to establish our true purpose. These help you uncover how you can impact the world in ways that light you up from the inside so, if you haven't established them yet, take the time now.

Purpose is a word that's mentioned often in life, but the Western world tends to confuse purpose with career, aspirations or goals, and this results in a lot of people feeling a lack of purpose, meaning or fulfilment or falling into the trap of the ego. Just as my purpose isn't to do musicals, yours isn't to be a cop, a doctor, a teacher, a hairdresser or any other profession. These are all careers, dependent on factors out of your control (opportunities, education, geographic location etc.), and none of those factors diminish your purpose. As American poet Michael Meade says on Instagram, 'Purpose is not an objective outside aim, goal or achievement trying to happen.'

Our purpose, our soul purpose, is interconnected with the essence of who we are when our masks are off. In Sanskrit, the word is *dharma*, and to fulfil our dharma is to live from and in our highest sense of truth. As such, soul purpose is never about filling or serving our egos. Purpose is intrinsic – it lives in our hearts and is something we want to share with the world ... the impact we want to have, however large or small. Therefore, purpose is always interconnected with service or giving. It comes from you, but it's not about you. Purpose gives us a deep and radiating sense of fulfilment. Pablo Picasso said it beautifully, 'The meaning of life is to find your gift. The purpose of life is to give it away.'

When a person is living purposefully, they want to share it in many ways because they bring that purpose into anything they choose. It doesn't have to be career-related. As long as there is a deep purpose behind it, it will be fulfilling and soulful. That is why true purpose is bound in service. Service is soul food – it nourishes all who engage in it. When we are rooted in service, sharing openly, freely and lovingly with the world, we can't help but feel full from the act of filling others up.

Our purpose may be to help or heal others. It could be to inspire change, to teach, to bring joy and laughter, to build, grow or fix things. It might be a combination of these or something completely different. The point is that the root of our purpose is far deeper than any goal, therefore your purpose can't be confined to one action, job title or career.

Purpose has a soulful centre, but the ways you pursue that purpose can be free and fluid. It may shift between various projects, offerings, jobs and careers throughout your life. Let's say your deepest purpose is to heal. Your thoughts likely go immediately to something in the medical or health field, but you could also serve that purpose by growing organic food for people, by writing music, through scientific or technological innovation, by serving coffees to tired people at 6 a.m., or by simply smiling at a stranger. In this sense, our true purpose in life is about gifting the world something that comes from your heart and sharing it with no expectations!

Of course, there may be specific actions we enjoy partaking in more than others, or goals and paths for our purpose that we prefer. I love nothing more than a big old sing with a 60-plus-piece orchestra firing on all cylinders behind me, but I don't feel more or less purposeful singing in an acoustically delicious concert hall than when I'm coaching clients, writing this book or sitting in the studio recording the *Behind The Mask* podcast. By listening to extraordinary people tell their stories openly and authentically, I have a small part to play in facilitating them being heard and felt. Equally purposeful is teaching, or having meaningful conversations with friends and family, or studying and learning from the many courses and workshops along the spiritual and philosophical path I've taken. Purposeful living and offering that purpose in service is acknowledging that life feels infinitely better when it's about what we can give to the world rather than what we can get from it.

Of course, this doesn't mean we should no longer receive from people or the world. Receiving is also a part of life, and we're not required to renounce receiving in order to sustain a purposeful life. Giving and receiving can co-exist, just like the non-ordinary and the ordinary world. Our duty as discerning individuals is to dance between those spaces.

The important takeaway is that purpose isn't outcome-driven, it's intention-driven. Looking at Sanskrit once again, the word for intention is *sankalpa*. That intention comes from a place of heart and soul. We then choose to offer that outwardly without expecting anything in return. If our intention is purely to get or receive, then we will always be chasing, and we will never have enough. But if our intention is to serve purposefully and, in the process, we wind up receiving something lovely, or it puts food on the table and pays our bills, or we become wealthy, then that's simply a beautiful by-product of sharing.

Finding our purpose in our heart story

We all carry a story. Not the glossy, edited one that we share to come across as good or perfect, but the one that is truthful, full of flaws and insecurities, vulnerabilities and imperfections – the one that carries our successes and our failings. This is our heart story, filled with pathos. It can be confronting to share but, when we own and fully embrace our heart story, its power is immeasurable. Often, the seed of our soul purpose lives inside the muck, the yuck and the beauty of our heart story.

During my early years as a performer, I can openly say that I predominantly thought about myself – what I was doing out there, how I was sounding, how I looked, how I felt, where my next gig was coming from. Me. Me. Me. I can attest that I failed to acknowledge the bigger picture of the productions I was in and people I shared them with. Of course, I made great friends who I'm eternally loyal to and who I care deeply about. And while I've always felt invested in the actors I share the stage with when I am performing, sometimes that investment was motivated by what they could give me or what the production might do for my career rather than genuine interest.

To be fair, part of reaching the height I did as a performing artist, working at an extremely high level, was enabled by selfishness, self-absorption, self-focused behaviour or narcissistic traits. These weren't consciously malicious ones, just blinkers-on and make-it-about-me stuff. But, after a while, something had to shift. That mindset neglected people who deserved my genuine, unconditional investment, and I realised my self-absorption was unsustainable and detrimental to all my relationships, personal and professional.

When I looked in the mirror and really acknowledged those patterns, it made me feel like shit. It made me question why I felt so caught up in my own stuff. Is there a less selfish way to do this career, or does success require me to wear thick masks and have a huge ego? What is my definition of success? Is there a higher purpose to it all? This current version doesn't feel right. I guess I was under the impression that the higher I climbed, the better I would feel, so I just kept climbing, one mountain to the next, one achievement after another. That's what I thought my career was about – what I thought success looked like. So, when Covid hit and I fell off that mountain, I started to ask myself some fairly deep and profound questions, the first of which was: What is my purpose?

In late 2020, living in chilly Brighton on the south coast of the UK, I pondered the question of purpose for several weeks. I would take it on my runs and bike rides through the streets, on my walks up and down the crisp, windy foreshore, and in my daily meditations. I came up with varying versions of the answer: to share music, to share stories, to express, to create. None of them were wrong, but they didn't feel like the full answer, the soul's answer.

One day, while upholding some rigorous social distancing in the park across from my apartment, I sat in meditation and recalled a conversation in Asher's 'The Way' course. The conversation was around living in the non-ordinary world to gain access to a deeper sense of feeling. That concept, which I discussed earlier, started bubbling away, then it dawned on me that that's really what I value most in life – connecting to the non-ordinary world. That's why I prefer to play rich and complex characters onstage. That's why I enjoy meditation, deep conversations and laughter that makes you wee a little. That's why I've dabbled in plant medicine and engage so unfailingly in spirituality, philosophy and poetry, the study of the human condition, and matters of the heart. Most importantly, this is how I could serve others. To help them feel the emotional and spiritual depths of themselves, and offer a taste of life behind the mask of the ordinary. There it was: the kernel of purpose, the biggest reason for it all.

Why did I want to share this with the world? Well, that part was simple. Nobody is immune to the human condition and to suffering. I thought that maybe I could help people make sense of it all, to navigate their way through life with greater meaning. Or perhaps I could at least pose some of those deeper philosophical and spiritual questions for their consideration. It felt like I had cracked myself open and inside was another me, just a lighter, fuller version.

It also occurred to me that my soul purpose wasn't specific to performing in any way – it was bigger than that. I suddenly felt this vast freedom that I didn't have to confine myself to a specific career to feel purposeful. Most importantly, my purpose wasn't about me at all. It offered me a way of zooming out from the tiny, insular, self-absorbed world I had created for myself in musical theatre and gave me the biggest and most important life lesson: life isn't about me and what I can get from it, it's really about what I can give and the impact I can have on others. This was a massive lightbulb moment for me!

I now see this time of reflection as my soul leading the way and that's why I needed to find greater meaning. We all ask ourselves at one time or another, What am I really here for? I believe that in awakening to our soul's purpose, we are a step closer to answering that question and to feeling truly alive.

A change is required

Living a life of purpose doesn't just happen by itself – we have to make a change. But if we are asleep at the wheel, currently discontented, stuck in the rat-race and a perpetual cycle of unfulfilling monotony, or we feel something is intrinsically missing from our lives, then what better time to start than now? Change is natural in life. If there was no change, we would still be bashing sticks together in the hope that a spark would eventually take care of our central heating.

Consider the humble caterpillar. When it builds a cocoon, there is an evolutionary and ecological realisation that its current form can no longer serve it. To transform, the caterpillar enters a process called 'metamorphosis', which lasts four weeks. On the other side of that process is a beautiful butterfly. But, like any transformation, it's not easy. There is a breaking down that needs to happen – the caterpillar is reduced entirely to goo then rebuilds itself from the same constituent parts. It makes something brand new out of itself without needing to add anything. It then rips through that cocoon and flies freely as a butterfly. We can do the same ... minus the goo.

Sometimes, as humans we need to break down in order to build back up with greater wisdom. This can involve some serious suffering but, as Buddha said, 'Life is suffering.' Nobody believes they deserve to suffer, but it's an inherent part of the human condition. It's not always the same, but everyone experiences it. Rather than trying to attach ourselves to our suffering or push it away, if we see our suffering through a lens of learning, we can use it as a vehicle for growth or even metamorphosis. We may not be consciously asking for it, and suffering may not necessarily be our fault, but we can adopt the philosophy that there is deeper wisdom to be gained from it. Once we start perceiving things this way, we become far less defined by our suffering and far more curious and capable of growing from it. We go aha!, that illness, that injury, that challenging person at work, that break-up, that breakdown, that confrontation, that fear, that shame, that pain – it's all grist for the mill ... it's all a teacher. And, through that suffering, we might just find our soul purpose.

Unfortunately, Western society places very little value on asking philosophical questions like 'What is my soul purpose?' There is very little support for people to enter that space of discovery. It's often something we are required to do alone. You may never have been asked what your purpose is, but I almost guarantee that, before you hit the age of ten, you were asked what you wanted to be when you grew up. Worse than that, answers like fulfilled, contented, loving, inspiring, joyous or free didn't answer the question the way people wanted it answered. They wanted to hear you say 'a fireman' or 'a footy player'. In fact, when my sister and I were young, my grandma used to take us on walks through the park. If she bumped into a friend and they asked who we were, my grandma would reply nonchalantly, 'This is "the doctor" and this is "the lawyer".' What hope did we have?

Society focuses heavily on what we do, rather than who we are. It reinforces measurement by extrinsic results rather than our intrinsic qualities, and we follow those rules obsessing over our human doing rather than focusing on the human being. So, it's not your fault that you've never considered your purpose from a heart or soul lens or something more than a career, job title, goal or achievement. And, as much as that sucks, and you may not be able to change society's misunderstanding of the difference between the human doing and the human being, you do have the power to change how you go about *your* life. By breaking down these expectations and the status quo, you begin asking yourself deeper questions. With curiosity, we don't just break down our relationships with the world and its systems – we begin to break through those thick layers of conditioning, the masks we've been wearing our whole lives. Getting behind those masks and finding the person beyond the persona is a part of our metamorphosis and, just like the butterfly whose purpose is to fly freely, in changing our relationship with who we truly are, we step onto the pathway of finding our true soul purpose.

For some people, finding their soul purpose can be a life's work – some never find it. There are a multitude of reasons, but generally it's because their focus is purely on what they can obtain from the extrinsic and material world rather than questioning what their intrinsic motivators might be and what they can give to the world. Regardless of why, their life hasn't asked them to look inward yet and, in my opinion, that is one of the deepest forms of suffering. By making the change to look inward and taking the first steps to finding your soul purpose, you're beginning to consider what I believe is a core component of what we are meant to realise in this lifetime.

Journal exercise: finding your soul purpose

Take this opportunity to reflect upon your 'heart story', the one you wrote during Chapter 1.

If you went soft the first time, let's add to it and include all the slings and arrows, bumps and bruises, successes and failures. Take some time now to write it out in your journal. It may be short and sweet, or several pages long.

Now add the times in your life where you felt like you had a positive impact on someone else.

What does this say about your life and what truly lights you up? Our heart stories tell us a lot about who we are but, more importantly, they give us a lens into what drives us, what we feel passionate about, what we want to share with others and how we want to serve in the world.

Take your time in writing all this down. This book isn't going anywhere, so you don't need to rush. Remember that soul purpose involves the soul, so it's slow and grounded. It's also a process that we come back to over the course of our lifetime, so even if you write everything down now, there will be more to come later. Keep journalling your reflections as you have them.

The important thing to recognise is that purpose is a seed that can be planted in many different places. It's never a specific job, title or career – the vehicles for sharing our purpose are interchangeable. If our purpose is to help, inspire, heal or teach, we can do that in infinite ways.

Once you've established your soul purpose, ask yourself why you've chosen this. Without fail, it will have something to do with serving others and having a positive impact on the world.

Serve and feed

When spiritual teacher Ram Dass stood before his guru Maharaji, he asked him, 'How can I know God?' Maharaji said, 'Feed people.' Unsure of how to respond, Ram Dass then asked, 'But how do I become enlightened?' to which Maharaji responded, 'Serve people.' To serve and feed people is to interact from the soul.

Serving and feeding doesn't need to be taken literally. As charitable and as just as it is, you don't have to work at a soup kitchen feeding the homeless and the food insecure to serve and feed. It can come in the form of so many different acts of service that may involve sharing your soul purpose, which is a beautiful way to serve. I'm not necessarily suggesting that you have to give money or donate items. This isn't about that. What I'm really suggesting is that you put your needs to one side and help another who is in need. Simple daily acts of service are grounded in compassion and in building stronger personal connections. That is the definition of charitable service – acts that serve relationships, feed the soul and alleviate another's suffering.

When we approach life in this way, we start to step into a more conscious state, one that is increasingly aware of the interconnection we have with all living things – a relationship that is compassionate and empathetic. As the executive director of Social Health Australia, Joe Sehee, says on season two of the BTM podcast, 'Compassion is suffering together.' When we are truly compassionate, we begin to feel that oneness between souls and we can't help but be compelled to be of service. This isn't because it's righteous or altruistic or because we want to be seen to be a nice or generous person, but because there is no other choice. We can't ignore another's suffering – that would make us suffer too. I think that's part of the reason we do feel good when alleviating another's suffering ... because, in the oneness of compassion, we are also alleviating the inherent suffering that exists within us.

Let's use another camp musical theatre reference to help make sense of all this. Let's say you have a friend who wants to audition for the local amateur production of *The Sound of Music*. They've never sung a note in their life, let alone solved a problem like Maria, and neither have you. They want to challenge themselves and step out of their comfort zone, but they're fretting over it and scared to do it alone. After seeing this vex them for a couple of weeks, you acknowledge that you can help to alleviate their suffering by giving it a crack as well. Can you imagine the look on their face when you tell them that you're auditioning with them? That iconic, pre-rehearsed high-five moment between the two of you when you both see your names on the cast list? The costume fitting when you try on your nun's outfits together for the first time and try to remember whether its 'testicles, spectacles', or the other way round? The watery glint in your eyes when you turn to each other during 'Climb Every Mountain' on closing night? The afterparty, where you both agree that not only is Steve cuter than Jack, but he has an infinitely better voice and was robbed of playing Rolf because Jack was sleeping with the choreographer during auditions. Then there's the hungover pact you make the next day to do this annually ... forever!

This one simple act of service has positively fed a relationship – this is what serving and feeding is all about. Compassionate acts that alleviate another's suffering are as simple as putting your needs aside to have a positive impact on someone else's. One simple act of serving and feeding can go a hell of a long way. This highly camp musical theatre experience felt right for the book, but it might apply to a fun run, an actual camp, a concert, a weekend away, a gym class or just being there – the possibilities to create experiences like this for another, and in turn yourself, are endless.

I've found in recent times that one of my greatest passions is to help young people. Having climbed a few mountains in my lifetime and career, I've reached a point where I've sat at the top enough. Right now, I'm far more interested in helping others walk up it for the first time.

In 2024, I took on two new roles: one was lecturing in musical theatre once a week, back at Federation University, Ballarat, where I studied many moons ago. The other was taking on a role as an ambassador for the Western Bulldogs Community Foundation. Both opportunities have been about helping young people on their journey up the mountain of life. With the musical theatre students, it comes in the form of their 'Acting Through Song' class, something that brings up a hell of a lot of insecurity and asks young performers to be incredibly open and vulnerable, trusting in their innate capacity to tell stories through challenging songs and subject matter. With the foundation, it's been working on public speaking with their youth leaders around the state. Once again, this is frightening and nerve-racking for 14-to-16-year-olds. Using the philosophies that I've shared in this book, I help them open up and get out of their own heads and out of their own way. I help them share their heart stories or their character freely and openly. I help them access the non-ordinary within them. It's so beautiful to watch them wade through their discomforts and challenges to those breakthrough moments, coming out the other side with new-found confidence and excitement. It's not about the money – much of it is pro bono – but rather the feeling of immense fulfilment. It makes my heart feel fuzzy and warm, and beyond the corporate landscape or coaching clients who have more lived experience, it's further vindication that these philosophies really do help people.

I hope you can now appreciate that service can come in many forms. It's in discovering your soul purpose and sharing it for the benefit of others, and it's in making the change to focus your intention on giving rather than receiving. It's in choosing to serve and feed, whether literally or figuratively. It can also be as simple as listening and hearing a friend or a person in need.

Recently, more and more people have started seeking me out in private to express what they're feeling, to get something off their chest, maybe to open up about something that's troubling them, or just to have a cry and be comforted. I might get a call from a friend or someone I mentor, or a student who wants to chat to me about an issue they're struggling with after class. It might be a client I coach one-on-one. The most powerful medicine is to do nothing but listen to them ... to really hear them. It's not to butt in with advice or my opinion, or to fix, judge or challenge them or tell them to behave differently. It's just to be a companion in the pit of their suffering – not trying to get them out of that pit but sitting in it with them. It's amazing how much better people feel after these moments. They say, 'Thank you so much for your help.' Initially, my response was, 'I didn't do anything', to which they often replied, 'Yes, you did.' We all want and need love – being there for someone in their grief, concern, stress or suffering is one of the most beautiful and powerful ways to share it and an equally powerful way to be of service.

Journal exercise: following your soul purpose

Now that you've established what your soul purpose is and why, how might you express that purpose? What sort of vehicles, actions or jobs might you choose to do that through? Does this require the courage to make a big change in your life? How will that change positively affect you and the people around you?

Can you let go of what you think you should do or what society/others say you need to do and instead serve from your intrinsic soul purpose? How can you 'serve and feed' to impact others in ways that are truly compassionate and that alleviate suffering?

These are some big questions, ones that may take time to answer. Be patient, ruminate on them, allow them to marinate and percolate within you. Answers to such big life questions can't be forced – they simply arise exactly as they need to. To help this, journal your thoughts and meditate on these questions often.

6

PART 6

Flow

The flow of life

As humans, we are made of energy, existing in and on a planet made of energy revolving around a sun that provides our planet with energy, in a solar system made up of ... energy. It's all energy. Infinite subatomic particles dancing around the universe and making up the universe.

When you expand your relationship with the universe and realise that everything is made of the same stuff, the same essence, you begin to see why Rumi said, 'You are not a drop in the ocean. You are the entire ocean in a drop.' That essence is energy. The energy we put out directly affects what comes back to us. We are the creators. We are the universe manifested in form, and we are always working in a symbiotic relationship with that which is universal. That relationship requires flow.

The idea of immersing ourselves in the flow of life is

an act of brave surrender. But there is a distinct difference between floating through life and allowing yourself to be a part of the flow of life. The former lacks intention, purpose and direction. There are no goals, dreams or desires. It's an evasive approach, devoid of responsibility, like letting someone randomly choose two scoops of ice cream for you. (We can't just sit back and allow tragedies like this to occur!) On the other hand, the latter is active and offers up the idea of an exchange ... an energetic exchange between us and the universe.

To stay within that flow requires balance and non-attachment. It asks you to remain in awareness: choosing when to go, when to stop, when to slow down, when to move quickly, when to shift and when to adapt, when to acknowledge that you are resisting and pushing against that energy, or when the ego has stepped in and you're conforming to the incessant fears, anxieties and neuroses of the mask and the thinking mind.

Practices like yoga, qigong and tai chi also require flow between the mind, the body and the breath and offer much wisdom to accessing and understanding the flow of life at a deeper level. They are steeped in tradition and philosophical and spiritual wisdom thousands of years old. For example, the definition of yoga is union, the union of mind, body, spirit and breath, and for me it has always felt like a balance or a flow between those things.

The older I've become, the more I've acknowledged my

flaws as a person, one of which is moving too fast. While sometimes moving quickly can work, for me, it's often a trap. There is need for harmony and balance in my life and moving more methodically and intentionally always serves me better.

I find that yoga is a beautiful mirror for my life and a great way to be reminded of when things are out of balance. When I'm struggling to find balance in a tree pose (a one-legged asana or position), chances are the tree of my life is unbalanced, so I take that as a sign to see where I might find some more balance. The yoga mat is more than a place to stretch – it's a place that is constantly asking me where I am physically, mentally, emotionally and spiritually. It's like a life check-in. Am I looking at other people in the class and seeing what they look like in their poses? Okay, where else is comparison showing up in my life? Am I getting pissed off at my inflexible body? Okay, where else is anger or frustration showing up in my life? Is my mind wandering and I'm not present with my breath? Okay, where else is distraction showing up for me off the mat? The wisdom is simple, yet infinite if you choose to see it and use it.

In all these practices, there is a common language. Yoga uses the word 'prana' (life force), tai chi and qigong use the word 'chi' or 'qi' (life force) – different words from different parts of the world that share identical meanings. They refer to the energy that flows through us and through everything. They refer to the flow of the universe, and they ask for a balance in all things. In Chinese philosophy, qi is the force of creation that binds everything in the universe. It is both everything and nothing. Just like the nothingness of the infinite expanse of the universe is also everything.

How fitting. Eastern cultures have always had a deeper understanding of the need for balance and we have much wisdom to learn from them. Like sitting in the ice to find surrender or meditating to become more discerning, these practices are wonderful methods to help us find flow in life. But they are just methods. There are no right or wrong methods, just the ones that work for us. You might find your method is cooking. The method is less important than the lessons.

So, in acknowledging the importance of flow, how do we tune into it? Let's take a deeper dive into where flow can take you, where the traps lie and how to intuitively stay on your path, acknowledging that the universe will always find a way of balancing things out.

We are the architects

Creativity is the language of the soul. When we are freely creating, we are in flow. That isn't to say we all have to be talented artists or performers waiting to star in the musical of our life story. Sorry to put a pin in that dream! But every day, every one of us is consciously or unconsciously the creative architect of our internal world, and this directly effects our external world and how we traverse within the bigger flow. This is why internal work is so important – it *will* manifest externally … it's up to you whether that's as a gift or a curse or something in-between.

Our internal worlds are commonly referred to as our thoughts, mindset and belief systems. Yes, much of this relates to our social conditioning and past experiences, positive or traumatic but, objectively speaking, nobody can shift or change our internal world other than ourselves. We may be inspired or motivated by others (if you've come this far, then hopefully this book is another piece of inspiration for you), but we're the only ones who can do the work if there's something that we acknowledge needs to shift.

Our internal world is inherently connected to our experiences of the external world. Simply put, if we wake up thinking it's gonna be a shit fight of a day, convince ourselves of this then act like it from 9 to 5, chances are we'll head home that night after work complaining to our partner or friends that it was just that … an absolute shit fight. And it's highly likely, based on our perception of immediate past experiences, that we now believe tomorrow's going to be more of the same. We're manifesting that experience through a rigid internal dialogue with no scope for any other option, and we have conditioned our thoughts, beliefs and mindset to hold that information as gospel.

Therefore, we have to acknowledge our power and thus our responsibility for what we consistently create: good, bad and everything in-between. That isn't to say the universe won't throw stones, rocks and boulders at us every now and then, even when everything is going swimmingly internally and externally. Crisis is inevitable. As I often say on my podcast, 'The extraordinary lived experiences of my guests are a constant reminder that life isn't about what happens to us – it's about how we respond to what happens to us.'

If we believe that we are coalescing with something greater than ourselves, we then begin to see how the universe might be testing us and see the opportunity for learning in almost every situation. Challenges, as discussed in Chapter 2, are our opportunity for growth. When we stop acting like the victim every time something doesn't go our way, we might instead ask, 'What can I learn from this? How is this here to help me to grow?' or 'What is this failing (or triumph) trying to teach me?' Ultimately a conscious being will see all wins, losses, pleasures, pains, successes and sufferings as a vehicle for further awakening.

We also start to acknowledge and own that our perception of our experiences is not an absolute truth, just one subjective truth. When we realise that what we believe is happening is just our perception, and not the only truth, we become less attached to our thoughts and belief systems, less inclined to blame others or situations for our plight and more inclined to discern subjectivity from objectivity. As a result, we take ownership of and responsibility for the role we play in both our sufferings and successes. Unpacking our internal worlds goes a long way to shifting our mindset –

when we change the way we look at things, the things we look at change.

Becoming the creative architect to manifest our goals and dreams into reality is one of the key components of the journey we have taken thus far. But is that just another way to satiate the ego, another mask to wear? Absolutely not – in fact, it's the opposite. Taking off our masks, stepping out of somebody training, embracing our fears, expanding our awareness, following our bliss and serving the world with our innate purpose allows us to dream as big as we want, to set goal after goal for ourselves knowing that who we are, our true 'I am', is beyond any result we may manifest. It gives us more power, currency and agency – we end up placing far less pressure on ourselves to achieve those goals, knowing our self-worth is not defined by them. This releases us from the shackles of pressures and expectations, and that shift is a recipe for freedom. It gamifies things, turns the music of life up and allows us to play in the dance. No, we don't know whether those dreams or goals will manifest into reality, but that doesn't stop us from having a red-hot crack.

Flow state

When we can truly live in the present, when we can fully experience a moment, everything changes. In some instances, we can almost take that moment with us.

Have you ever felt like you've been lost in a time vortex, where half an hour felt like five minutes? If yes, then chances are you were either balls deep in the hippy movement of the 60s (all credit to you) or you were in a flow state. I can't speak personally about the hippy movement (although let's face it, I would've loved it) but flow state is something I can speak about from many firsthand experiences.

Flow state is a place of pure, present-moment awareness that blends focus and freedom. When we are so invested in a single task and have no concern for a particular result or outcome, we move beyond the limitation of our thinking minds into a deeper, more expansive place. We stop policing and analysing the situation or ourselves – we transcend both chronological time and the thinking mind.

Athletes, creatives and entrepreneurs experience this state all the time – they refer to it as being 'in the zone'. It happens when they have confidence and trust in their skills and surrender to the flow of the moment. Meditation techniques which use a mantra, a sacred sound that, when gently and effortlessly repeated, help the conscious mind transcend to the infinite expanse of the subconscious. As these techniques ask for complete surrender, they've become a very useful tool to help me regularly access flow state.

Many times throughout my career, I felt like I've transcended to another place. I think the act of singing, the vibration and the flow of breath that enables that vibration to move through a space, is a potential doorway to flow state, both for artists and audiences. There is a synergy between the breath, the heart, the voice, the music and the universe that creates something magical when it's in sync. I know it has happened in countless performances of 'Music of the Night'. Every time it has happened, I remember very little, if any, of the performance. Anything I try generally just works, because why shouldn't it? Flow state is when we are so comfortable and confident in what we are doing that we flow with complete and utter freedom – we are keenly focused but without tension. It's a beautiful dance at the intersection between something worldly and something truly divine.

Plant medicine

Similarly, when I've taken psilocybin, I've explored those states of flow and transcendence. I absolutely do not advocate for anyone acting illegally or doing anything they don't want to do. I am choosing to share my journey with you – in Australia, an authorised psychiatrist can supervise their patients through a psilocybin journey.

Psilocybin has taken me to other planes of consciousness where I've experienced something otherworldly. Yes, I've meditated for years and that is enough to cultivate profound experiences of transcendence. I was just curious about where psilocybin could take my sense of awareness, and those first few mushroom experiences opened me up to worlds beyond the world I knew. Thankfully, it never weirded me out (that phrase has a whole new meaning now: out of tune with the intersection of the two worlds). I was 100 per cent ready for it, which I think is the most important part; bringing fear into a psychedelic journey is a bad idea. You have to have a clear intention. Exploring psilocybin as sacred medicine opened me up to sensory experiences and a oneness (especially with nature) well beyond basic human sensory experiences. If the television of my life had been operating on analogue (well, probably digital), psilocybin gave me access to a host of streaming platforms.

I remember an experience I had on a farm in the UK, where I lay in a field on the grass and watched on with awe as the trees turned a colour I had never seen before. They didn't turn orange and purple or have cashed-up bearded leprechauns flying out of them, but every nuance and varied detail of green I could possibly imagine was on offer. I just lay there, so fascinated by it all, as if I was a child witnessing something for the first time. A gentle breeze picked up, and the leaves of the trees danced in slow motion with it, as if the earth was enjoying its relationship with the air. There was a oneness to it all. I was a part of the dance between the wind, the trees, the sky and the grass, and I felt my heart connect to it all in what can only be described as *love*. In its sacred way, psilocybin opened up my heart to truly loving all that is nature. Time as I knew it stood still. I must have been in that field for hours, but it felt like minutes. I can see why psychedelics are being used to treat anxiety and depression – they are a gateway to the present moment.

I also remember another, very different, experience. I was

at a kirtan, a music and mantra call-and-response singing style of meditation. I had taken a dose before attending to see how it would manifest beyond my usual sensory perception of live music. As the plant medicine took its course, I closed my eyes. It was like I was traversing through the pits of hell, wading through fire and demons that were laughing and gawking at me. There was the usual brimstone and boiling pits of lava – it was very fucked up! I'm sure demonic experiences like this are the reason why a lot of people shy away from trying psychedelics. For a short time, maybe five or forty-five minutes (I'm not sure, I had transcended time) that experience scared the living shit out of me. But then my awareness kicked in, and I realised that this was just a movie playing out in my mind. I became aware that I wasn't the movie, rather the screen on which the movie was being played. As that feeling became more expansive, I began to laugh at myself, then the movie changed and I was back experiencing the kirtan. The waves of music turned into colours and shapes and it was epic and wild, indescribable in the most magical way. I got to experience music in colour and shapes and that blew my mind!

A lot of people are afraid of the idea of visiting those other planes and they reduce it to, 'Oh, you're just hallucinating or tripping out!' And while I'm not telling anyone to do anything they don't want to do, I'm offering the thought that from my experience, this wasn't so much of a tripping out but a tripping in – into deeper parts of myself, to collective consciousness, to a greater sense of symbiosis, to truth, beauty and love.

Most people disregard this and see it as woo-woo or nonsense. But that dismissal is usually just people needing to maintain control. When we do that, we are saying that can't be a reality because it's not my reality. But it *is* reality – I and many others have experienced it over thousands of years. We may not fully understand it, but that's not necessarily a reason to shun it, reduce it or diminish it.

Once again, I don't advocate doing anything illegal. We are free to make our own conscious choices, and there are medical professionals to guide people through psilocybin journeys in this country. Psilocybin is now being used to treat depression and anxiety in instances where someone is resistant to traditional medical treatments. Those who might find themselves judging me sharing my experiences and support of psilocybin for mental health reasons might benefit from asking themselves where that judgement truly stems from.

Plot the destination, then ditch the map

If you're a self-help book buff like me, at some stage you've probably read '00s bestseller *The Secret*. If not, it's a 101 class in manifesting and the law of attraction. Looking back on it now, it's a bit of a basic approach. Cue the cheesy '90s American infomercial accent – 'I wanted the red bike, so I put a photo of it up on my bedroom wall, and that

Christmas it magically appeared.' There's a little more to it than that, but it basically offers up the theory that what you are seeking is seeking you and that the universe is always conspiring to say yes.

True manifestation requires non-attachment and a hell of a lot of surrender. You have to acknowledge that, sure, there are challenges and adversities that nobody is immune to, but those challenges also ask us to be malleable and flow in possibly many new directions to reach a goal. You might have a destination in mind, a specific goal or dream you want to achieve, but nobody can ever map out the course. You can decide what you want, but not necessarily how you'll get there. As Stoic philosopher Marcus Aurelius said, 'What stands in the way becomes the way.'

In approaching our life journey with flow, we are saying that, regardless of what's thrown at us, we get a say in where that journey goes and how it looks. We're not discouraged or disrupted by one or two roadblocks – we can still be adaptable and choose an alternate path, one that flows more freely. We still have power. But, as we know, with great power comes great responsibility. It requires us to own all of our choices, actions and responses, as all of those micro moments directly impact the macro. Take this moment to reflect upon the ups and downs of your life and the role you played in all those moments. This could be a lot to take in. It could be an opportunity for you to really celebrate yourself and your successes or it might be so triggering that you decide to burn every page of this book!

So, while you're pondering that, let me share a personal story to help give you a better sense of how powerful our capacity for manifestation is when we fearlessly follow the flow with a clear ability to respond (response-ability).

I love crystals. My apartment is full of them, and I often wear them around my neck. In January 2019, I attended a crystal mandala-making workshop. Apart from creating beautiful mandalas, we were asked to write one word on a cut-out card shaped like a leaf that Ash, the facilitator, handed to everyone in the room. We needed to write something that we wanted to manifest into our lives for that year. We were told that the previous year was a challenging one for many people, but 2019 would be a powerful year, so we should choose wisely. For me, the leaf meant that whatever I wrote down was going to be taken in the breezy flow of manifestation.

At this stage, I hadn't auditioned for *The Phantom of the Opera* in London. I didn't even have an audition in the works. I was living in Melbourne, having just returned from a trip to Europe. I was going about my Aussie life, but something inside me said, 'Be fearless, be brave, this is the role you've always wanted to do. Write that down and put that dream out into the universe.'

Often, the biggest hurdle standing in the way of us manifesting dreams into reality is our self-limiting beliefs, our fear that we don't deserve something, that we aren't good enough or capable enough. Maybe we fear what life would look like if we actually realised our dreams so we avoid going after them. In this particular moment, I believed wholeheartedly that this dream could be a reality, so rather than asking, 'Why?' and giving a thousand reasons why it wouldn't happen, I said, 'Why not?' Taking it out of my head and heart by writing it down and putting it out into the universe set the wheels in motion. I had planted the seed; now it was just a matter of watering it.

The universe doesn't operate in the future or the past, only the present, like us. So, when we manifest, we only need to put the dream out once – from then on, we need to believe that it is already realised. That's how it works. The paradox is that we need to be unattached to the goals we're manifesting. We need to know that if they don't come off, the universe is still conspiring in our favour. It's a fatalistic way to operate, but for me it always feels like there's a flow. Anytime I've pushed against that flow, it's never worked out.

You know when you feel that flow, because everything begins conspiring in your favour. You start seeing signs everywhere, and life almost feels like a game. But even games have rules and require structure. So, once I had made that decision that I was going after this dream, I decided to make some plans. Manifestation is incredibly powerful. It isn't just about having an idea, writing it down and expecting it to magically come to fruition. It also asks you to work for it. For me, that meant working out the space between playing the Phantom and where I was in that moment.

No, I didn't have an audition, which was vital, but I trusted one would come when the time was right. What I did have was the full score to the show. What's the universe telling me? Learn the score. I called my good friend, musical director Guy Simpson, and asked him if he was happy to coach me on the material. Guy had worked on the show for decades internationally as musical director, conductor and now as the musical supervisor. He knew everything there was to know about the show musically. He agreed to help.

Guy is unequivocally 'no bullshit'. In that first session, he gave me some fairly harsh feedback about not being prepared (circle back to the five P's). I recall it vividly. He asked me if I knew the main song, 'Music of the Night'. It's a standard that I had sung many times before on cruise ships and at corporate events, so I said, 'Of course, I've sung it heaps. Let's just give it a whirl, shall we?' I hadn't prepared at all. Guy sat at the piano and began playing the opening phrases. I got through the opening line before he stopped me and asked me to try again. The second time I got through the opening two lines before he closed his score, told me I don't know it at all and asked me to come back once I had properly prepared. A harsh truth. The universe was asking me how badly I really wanted this.

It turns out I wanted it very badly. So, knowing nothing comes for free, I sat down and really went to work on it.

I had learned my lesson and decided to learn the entire score, every single note, every word. Everything that could be learned, I learned, and not just learned – obsessed over. I began to play out the scenes in my living room, finding nuance and depth to the complex, flawed masked genius. I was in tears on my living room floor playing out the final scene. My neighbours probably thought I was having some sort of musical breakdown! I returned to Guy after weeks of diligence and, acknowledging how much time and energy I had put into it, we began exploring it all in greater detail. He told me what I would need to perform it if I was to audition at some stage. Whenever that was, I felt ready.

In the meantime, the universe was working away, doing its thing, conspiring to say yes. I had performed 'Nessun Dorma' on TV (remember the fear that I needed to move through?) not long before, and the footage had wound up in the email inbox of the London casting director for *Phantom* (I believe even Andrew Lloyd Webber and Cameron Mackintosh saw it). They reached out and said that if I was ever in London, they would accommodate me with a general audition. I got on the next flight I could.

I auditioned, returned home, flew back over for more auditions a few months later, then some more and, on 9 September 2019, nine months after writing on that leaf, I was playing the Phantom on London's West End.

This was all a grounding reminder of the power of manifestation and trusting the flow. On a side note, the colours I used on that mandala are the exact same as the Phantom's mandarin jacket that he wears in Act 1.

Sometimes I wonder what would have happened if this hadn't worked for me, if playing the Phantom didn't manifest. Would that have changed my belief systems? Would I have thrown my mandala out the window!? No, not at all. Firstly, I would've been fine. Sure, there would've been the obvious disappointment at not getting the role this time, but part of doing this work is trusting that the universe is always conspiring to give you exactly what you need.

The other important part to acknowledge is the lesson of how doing the hard work always serves you regardless. I am generally a diligent person. I've never considered myself exceptionally talented, my talent seed was actually quite small. I just chose to give it some serious TLC (my classmates at university will vouch for that). But I've always been a disciplined, dedicated and meticulous hard worker. We all need a kick in the bum every now and then – I'm no exception, and Guy gave me a solid one. But when there's something I really want to do, I stop at nothing to find little improvements, often working on boring and laborious nuances and details, like how a single note can flower and bloom and how that crescendo almost has a life of its own. How a tiny inflection on a single syllable changes and affects an entire phrase, an entire passage, a character's wants, desires and needs. I go to the nth degree. For me, it's an athlete's mindset of leaving no stone unturned and committing wholeheartedly to improve in everything I set out to do.

Some people may call my story good luck, serendipity, making the most of opportunities or simply a series of timely coincidences. There's a saying of spurious origin: 'The harder I work, the luckier I get.' I may have been lucky with some of my achievements, but I worked bloody hard to be that lucky. I feel that people say things like this to reduce achievements so that narrow-minded people can try to stay in control or to define that which cannot be defined, as if having a clear answer to a situation, like dismissing it, means we don't have to be open to the possibility that we don't understand what causes it. That sounds pretty arrogant to me. We've all had those moments where we're thinking about someone, and soon after that they text or call. Is it all coincidental, or is there an energetic flow at play? If we are open to the latter, to the idea that maybe our universe is operating on frequencies and energy beyond the limitations of our human sensory experiences, then we are choosing to play in that realm.

So, if you're coming to play, what do you want to experience? What goals and dreams do you want to put out there? How do you want to flow with life? What dream do you want to realise? Manifestation doesn't just have to be about your career – it might be relationships, finances or other experiences you want to bring into your life. However, it requires you to be incredibly specific and precise. The universe loves specificity.

Journal exercise: manifesting

Start by closing your eyes and connecting to your breath. Focus on extending the exhale, in and out, longer and longer each time. Once you feel settled and connected to your breath, begin to draw your attention to that space in the middle of your chest, your heart space. If distractions come, notice them then gently bring your awareness back to your heart space.

Now begin to listen to the small voice inside you, the intuitive voice. Wade through the temptation of the ego's voice or the persuasive thought that might just be telling you that you want some possession, something to fill you up quickly, something from the confectionery aisle in the supermarket.

Manifestation flows far easier when it not only comes from our soul purpose but from a place of fullness, rather than scarcity. It may take several days, weeks or even months until that little voice is louder than the loud voice. Keep practising this part of the meditation.

Once it arrives, you will know. It will be a deep knowing. It will feel unequivocally right, even if a bit scary. In fact, if it doesn't scare you a little bit, it's probably not right. I'm not suggesting it should be a nightmare, but our dreams should scare us in a way that challenges us.

Now write it down, one word or phrase that sums up what you want to manifest. Be specific. Then never write it again.

From then refer to it, whether in your thoughts, meditations or conversations, only in the present tense. Be sure to attach no self-worth to it. You are not dependent on this – it may be a good addition but it doesn't define your worth. It is there as a vehicle for you to share and serve your soul purpose. If it's meant to be, it will be – if it's not, something else is. That is the art of manifesting with flow. As Rumi said, 'As you start to walk the way, the way appears.'

Good luck, and happy manifesting!

Courage to heed the call

Generally, questions around identity, self-limiting beliefs, the absence of bliss and the need for greater purpose arise when we experience an intense personal crisis, maybe even an existential one. Suffering or a depression of any kind asks for change. And, if we want something to change, we have to change something ... more often than not, something within us. If we're courageous enough to make that change, we are awakening to the bigger self, the soul self. In that awakening, there is also a need to see and to listen to the bigger calls around us and for the immense courage to heed that call.

Since humankind has existed, we have tried to describe that bigger calling, but I like to call it a conversation with the universe. The universe is always speaking to us, always sending signs, always communicating. The universe is loving in nature, but it's very busy – it's got universing to do, it's not gonna sit there and wait for you to choose your long-weekend wardrobe, fold your clothes neatly, pack your toiletries (don't forget your toothbrush) and lock your suitcase. It expects you to be ready to go in that present moment. That's where it lives. Thankfully, the universe is consistent in its love, and those signs will continue to present themselves throughout your life's journey – that's how it flows. Therefore, it's not a matter of whether the signs arrive or not, it's a matter of whether you have the capacity to see them and the courage to heed the call.

If we think of our universe as a river, there is a natural current that flows strongest. Going where the river flows is just another way of saying you are listening to the bigger calling of the universe and leaning into it. The opposite would be to follow the ego's path and swim upstream against the current. We've all done that before. The ego thinks it's a pretty kick-arse swimmer, like Michael Phelps in his heyday! It is convinced it can achieve any goal, even if it's upstream, and it does everything in its power to get there. It might be swimming on the spot against the mighty current, not making any progress, bashing up against the rocks, the roots, the logs, the snags, but still it keeps fighting, kicking its legs, trying harder and harder to get to that destination.

Sometimes, it's strong enough to reach that goal and get a win. Then, before it's had time to stop and reflect on the journey, it sees another goal upstream and it has to go again. This is the only way it knows. It's only fed by one source, winning, and it's perpetually starving.

Eventually, the ego is inevitably exhausted. It's had enough, it's burnt out, it needs to step out of the river and take stock. It's upset about not reaching that next destination, sitting there on the bank like a victim. Rage builds up as it focuses its anger like a laser beam at the rocks, the roots, the logs, the snags, and the speed of the current, everything that got in its way. It hates not getting what it wants, it can't bear being hungry, and so it suffers. It wallows in its suffering for days, months, years.

Then, one day, the blame stops. There is a stillness and, rather than projecting everything outward, rather than getting angry or despondent or wallowing in victimhood, a courageous decision is made to go inward. Instead of looking despairingly upstream, it looks curiously downstream and, in doing so, it realises it wasn't the river's fault at all. The river was just being the river, the universe was just being the universe. There has been so much learning, so much wisdom gained from the fighting, the anger, the suffering, the victimhood, the ordeal and the scars to show for it. You realise how much energy you have wasted going against the flow.

Surrendering to the natural flow of the river, to the flow of life, is a surrendering to the soul's journey. The ego wants to get, but the soul wants to give. By turning inward then swimming downstream, the focus naturally shifts.

I've been that guy swimming upstream several times in my life and career and I've experienced all those sufferings of the ego: shame, blame, anger, wallow, victimhood, you name it. The last time was performing in *Les Misérables*. The feather, brick and train of that journey was a battle for my ego. Sure, there were countless moments of wonder, thrill, fun, excitement and pride, but I was exhausted after the run of *Phantom* in Australia, which finished a week prior to starting at *Les Misérables* (remember these aren't small roles), and I equally felt that I had a big point to prove.

Towards the end of my *Phantom* run in Melbourne in early 2023, after approximately 400 performances of the role, our producer, Sir Cameron Mackintosh, flew in from London to see our Australian production. This was the first time he had seen me play the role (the only other opportunity was the birthday show ... whoops!). I was understandably nervous. I felt the weight of expectation and pressure to deliver a version of my performance that lived up to the hype of the fantastic reviews and comments about what I had been doing with the role for the past three and a half years.

I let it get to me. It wasn't a perfect show, and it wasn't my best version of 'Music of the Night'. I was shaky and nervy, and my final note was particularly ordinary. But it was fine, and I warmed up as the show progressed. Some days later, Cameron asked me for brunch. I thought it was going to be a fun get-together, discussing ideas around *Les Misérables*, which I was to begin rehearsing in a few weeks. It was anything but that. Cameron was unapologetic in letting me know how disappointed he was with my performance and how I had a hell of a lot of work to do, especially vocally, if I was to cut it as Jean Valjean. This was ego-crushing, and it sat with me painfully for months and months. Should I have stood up to him, been firmer, let him have a piece of my mind? Should I have accepted his comments with more grace and understanding and calmly taken them all on the chin? I hadn't done either – instead I just let the criticism fester away.

So, by the time *Les Mis* was up and running and after the first injury had settled, I felt I was nailing it. I was proving myself to Cameron Mackintosh and his team, which kept me swimming against the tide of my physical, mental and emotional fatigue: my burnout. I remember Cameron coming to the show to decide if I was going to get another contract. I was like a prize-fighter that night. I took the months of pent-up frustration, shame and disappointment around my nervous Phantom performance and went out there, leaving nothing on the table. It was one of the fiercest, most focused and unapologetic performances I've ever given. Sure, there was a lot of ego in that, but I absolutely bled out there.

After the performance, Cameron came to my dressing room and, after making some flippant comment about my wig, gave me the compliments I had been craving for months. I put him on the spot right there and then to be re-contracted (I'm not sure that's happened before), and he immediately said yes. I should have taken my dad's heart surgery as a sign – I didn't need to stay on. I knew I was cooked, but this was ego, and my ego needed it. I needed that shot of validation after the brunch that went badly. It was a war between my soul purpose and my ego: a war between service and suffering. And we know what happened shortly after – it wasn't meant to be. I've learned huge lessons from this one. It's all a part of the journey, a part of being a student of life, a study that never stops. In the end, I'm so glad I let my ego fade and had the courage to heed the bigger calling, a necessary return home.

Trust, patience, sacrifice, laughter and giving it your all

In the stopping and reflecting and the quiet, I've learned so much and fully accepted how things panned out. Subsequently, even with its personal and family challenges, life has had a hell of a lot more flow since returning home to Australia. Swimming with the flow has enabled me to meet some amazing people, and I've had the opportunity to help many more along the way. I feel like I'm truly serving my soul purpose and having a positive impact on others through the podcast, through singing and music, through coaching and facilitating, through sharing stories and through various beautiful charity organisations I get to work closely with. It's all happening for you, the good bad and the ugly, even if you can't quite see it in the moment. In time everything tends to make sense of itself. As Asher says on the BTM podcast, 'You have to swim through the mud before you can walk on water.'

It's important to note that even flowing with the flow of the river doesn't mean you don't get the odd graze, bump or big knock. A soulful path or offering our purpose to the world from a place of service doesn't render us immune to life's challenges, stresses, pains, hurdles and sufferings, but it does give us a stronger reason to wake up every morning, a gravitas in knowing we are making a difference to the world, however small or large – that our life is alive with meaning and it is positively impacting others.

Furthermore, a soulful path doesn't stop our desire to reach destinations or to have goals or big dreams. But when our goals and dreams are rooted in purpose, suddenly there is a *why* to our *what.* That's why, when we serve and have an impact on others and there is no longer a fight with the ego, we can swim with the current and still enjoy the destinations along the way. We are no longer just doing it because we've been told we should do it or because of the major kick the ego can get from doing it.

Trust is probably the hardest thing to reconcile when trying to stay in flow. It asks us to let go of attachments and control, to be adaptable and malleable rather than holding onto our ideas and projections for the future too tightly. But this is crucial for manifesting a life of flow. The other part of trust is trusting ourselves – we have to trust that everything we need is already inside us. We shouldn't put conditions on or have self-limiting beliefs about our dreams if we know deep down that we're putting in the hard yards. Sure, we can't be deluded, our dreams have to align with our soul purpose and be grounded in reality. I can dream of singing alongside a million dancing hermit crabs in a theatre on Mars, but as clearly as I manifest, as much as I trust and as in flow as I feel, it ain't fuckin' happening! If you keep your dreams aligned to your purpose, and operate from fullness rather than lack, you will always flow in the right direction, even if you go in a direction you didn't think of originally. Trust the flow.

The second thing people struggle with when it comes to manifestation and flow is **patience**. We are becoming more immediate and entitled as a society. We want it now and believe we deserve it now. I'm not just having a dig at gen Z here – online shopping and delivery services aren't helping this, and neither is the immediacy of recognition through social media. However, manifesting requires you to be patient and let things unfold. I told you the story of *Phantom* happening in nine months. That's not entirely true – it really took thirteen years. I first auditioned for the show in 2006, made it to the last round and got cut. I next auditioned for it two years later. I was cast as an understudy but couldn't exit an existing contract I had with *The Ten Tenors*. Same goes for *Les Misérables* – I first auditioned in 2012 and was cut first round. In 2013, I was cut again in the second round. These were both dreams of mine from the age of sixteen. Big dreams take time to come to fruition. Be prepared to ride the ups and downs of patience.

Also, dreams will rarely be realised with a **half-arsed attitude**. Hard work is the space between talent and fulfilling your potential – between where you are now and where you want to be. There are the seeds of talent in all people, but if we don't water that seed, give it sunlight and food, it doesn't grow. This applies to all aspects of life, not just careers. On the topic of career, however, I've never been one for having plan Bs. I don't believe in them. I think they are a way of conceding before we even start playing the game. I am for having more than one plan A, though. If you're gonna do it, fucking do it, don't half-arse it. Don't regret anything you could've done. Don't leave any stone unturned. If it doesn't work out, that's cool, accept the flow of the universe and give your all to the next plan A. If we circle back to the idea of the ordinary and non-ordinary worlds, non-ordinary is the manifesting, and the hard, consistent, rigorous work is the ordinary. Sitting at the intersection is where we do our best work ... weirdo!

Some people are willing and prepared to put big dreams out into the universe, with real trust, and they're happy to wait it out patiently. But they forget that big dreams don't come freely – there is always a balance. These dreams inherently require **sacrifice**. If you put all your eggs in one basket, you won't have eggs for the other baskets. You can have it all, but you can't have it all at once.

So, the first thing to ask ourselves when putting our dreams out there is simple: Is this really what I want? Would I really be prepared to sacrifice many other things, even temporarily, when that dream becomes a reality? Sacrifice is an inherent part of life and an even bigger part of dreaming big and having success. If you're aiming for something big, know that it will come at a cost. For me, a big career has meant sacrificing time spent with family, in relationships and with friends. I've missed weddings, bucks parties, birthdays and so many other important events as well as all the tiny simple moments that end up being the most meaningful, because I was onstage or performing in another state or country and couldn't make it. Yes, I had some big dreams, but as I close in on forty and feel the beginning of middle age, I've realised that I've sacrificed enough for those dreams. As wonderful as those moments were, and as grateful as I am for those experiences, there are other things I value just as much, if not more. Friends and family are at the top of that list. I no longer want so many eggs in one basket – I'd like to spread them around.

The other thing that helps us stay in the flow as we work towards our goals and dreams is **laughter**. We can't take ourselves too seriously. There is a presence to laughter, a nowness. Throughout this book, I've constantly made light of things, ensuring there was a bit of comedy in what can be confronting and heavy subject matter. This is something I value: the ability to laugh at myself and situations, to laugh with people (not so much at them, but sometimes we do a bit of that too! Nothing like some schadenfreude). It's all a part of the dance of life, what is described in Sanskrit as *lila* – the play within life. I think laughter brings us back into balance. Ultimately, we all end up in the same place, so why not take it a bit less seriously, enjoy the game of it, be a shmuck, self-deprecate, get tickled and piss yourself laughing. It's far more fun that way! And, from my experience in making dreams come true, realising them never felt the same without a hell of a lot of laughter along the way.

Remember, what is for you won't pass you, so don't hold onto dreams too tightly ... you wind up crushing them. Be clear with your manifestation meditation and listen to that voice in your heart, the place where our soul's purpose lives. Once you've got that clear dream, write it down, but know that it may take you somewhere else or that you may arrive from a path you didn't expect. Flow with it, acknowledging the need for trust, patience, hard work, sacrifice and laughter.

The oneness of true love

As you have traversed through the pages of this book, you have asked yourself some of the most important existential questions we face in our lifetimes: Who am I and what are my core values? What do I want and why? What's my soul purpose and how can I serve with it? But the answers to these questions carry far less meaning without love.

This chapter could have started the book, and we would have been done and dusted pretty early, but I've waited until the end because it's the culmination of all the other chapters, stories and exercises. Every page has walked you along the path of understanding so you can freely open the gates to this final instalment. Choosing love, true love, is the hardest thing for us to do. We are constantly fed versions of love online, in the media, in books and in films. But so often these versions aren't real. They are not fully loving. They are conditional forms of love – the antithesis of unconditional love. But I can't stand that phrase. It's a contradiction in terms. Love in its very essence is unconditional. How can you half love or sort of love someone? (I'd argue that's likely lust.) Then there's the love for someone if and when they do something on your terms. Once again, that's conditional. That's selfish greed and the ego needing to be fed.

If you want to learn about love, spend some time with a dog. They don't do conditional love – they just love. The moment you get home, they love. When you're happy, they love; when you're sad, they love; when you're on the couch, they love; when you realise you forgot to feed them, they still love. So, for me, there is love and there isn't love. Love is pure – it's not academic. It's not born in the mind or the ego: it lives in the heart.

Author bell hooks shares in her *New York Times* bestseller, *All About Love*, a quote that was inspired by M.Scott Peck's poem *The Road Less Travelled*: 'Love is the will to nurture one's own or another's spiritual growth.' That will requires immense bravery and vulnerability, for love is the opposite of fear. Where love connects, fear separates, so to choose true love is therefore an acceptance of connection with everyone and everything. A loving oneness with the entire universe.

This is an improbable thing for so many of us to fathom and boy, do I stuff up all the time. But that doesn't stop me from trying. For choosing true love is ultimately about prioritising authenticity in its highest form – being true and loving to who we are, to all our relationships and in all encounters. Even with strangers. But it doesn't stop there. It asks us to choose love with people we think we might hate (insert several unnamed politicians). It asks us to find the part of them that we can still love. It doesn't say you can't despise someone's actions, but it asks you to view the soul behind the human, to compassionately acknowledge the human suffering behind those actions, whether seen or unseen. Moreover, it asks us to love everything: a fish, a bug, a tree, a cat, the sun, the moon, every bit of nature, every sentient being, everything that makes up everything. That is universal. I know, true love is big!

When the mind is transcended in deep presence and we access that space of expansive awareness, we enter what mystical Hinduism refers to as 'turiyia', or the fourth state of consciousness. In this state, duality, or the feeling of separateness, disappears. This doesn't mean that the reality of our day-to-day lives is false or some sort of illusion. On the contrary, the illusion is the false sense of separateness between us and other things.

The world, as most people see it, is just oneness appearing as separateness. Often, we see nature, people and other sentient beings as different or separate to us. This is the illusion. As previously mentioned, at a subatomic level, everything in the universe is made up of the same stuff, the same energy; it is all a part of the oneness. Therefore, both through a lens of physics or spiritually, there is oneness, and that oneness manifests as true love. As Ram Dass said, 'Love coalesces the universe. The oneness of the universe is love.'

True love is the energy of the universe singing together in perfect harmony through the beauty of oneness. But that oneness can turn into duality very quickly when the ego consciously or unconsciously enters into separateness. That's just a part of the play – humanness doing its human thing. The thinking mind gravitates towards separateness and duality. Black and white, good and evil, positive and negative. Duality is an inherent part of life, but it also plays into our need to be right or righteous, to feel in control. And that creates separateness.

Therefore, we must consistently choose to step back into oneness, into true love, even if we know we'll forever be dancing back and forth between the two. This choice asks us to relinquish our fears, our biases, our judgements, our projections and prejudices, parts of our conditioning and our desire to control. To see other souls beyond the physical and/or psychological form which, in turn, asks us to see ourselves in the same way. In doing so we move into the heart and surrender to the sacred, divine, and infinite. We surrender to oneness. Connecting back to oneness enables us to fully explore the bliss, the joy, the wonder and the magnificent boundless expanse of the fullest heart of a spiritual being. To choose true love is therefore a choice to embrace who we are, behind the mask.

Acknowledgements

This book was not conceptualised in its entirety before I put pen to paper, or rather before my fingers touched the keyboard. Like any creative pursuit, it was born from the moment an idea sparked in mid-2023, and remained alive until my wonderful publishing company forbid me from editing or adding anything to it a few months ago. For me, the writing process was like tending to a garden. The theories, ideas, concepts, anecdotes and stories, which all began as seedlings, were constantly tended to, nurtured and loved, and this helped the garden to grow naturally in its own unique way. Although the six parts are built on a solid framework, much of which has existed for thousands of years, many passages felt like they formulated themselves, and gave life to new passages, which birthed paragraphs, chapters and so on. Writing this book was both catharsis and vindication, as the concepts have been continually road-tested in real life teaching and coaching situations with immense success. This only solidified philosophical and spiritual theories I've been both pondering and embodying for many years. But while I am now thirty-nine, the garden is still very much alive and growing, and I know I'll have so much more to write about as the years and decades progress.

The are so many people I'd like to acknowledge and thank, who have played such pivotal roles in this book coming to life. Firstly, thank you to Echo Publishing for getting behind me and my ideas, and for wholeheartedly believing that there is a space in the world for a book like this.

To my beloved family. My parents, Hannah and Leon Piterman, my sister Lara, brother-in-law Nick, and my nephews, Rafael and Isaiah Karasavvidis. Thank you for being an endless source of inspiration and encouragement and for allowing me to annoy you at various stages throughout the process with a scrappy chapter or an unformed idea.

To my great friends who I loyally love and adore. You, my closest mates, know exactly who you are and have watched not only this idea grow, but all my iterations and undulations on the path of life and shown me love continuously in the most beautiful and honest ways.

To all my loving relationships and the flames that didn't last. Thank you for every lesson you've taught me and for challenging me to be a better man.

To my beautiful family overseas, especially Doris, Sophie,

Joe, David and Kate Naftalin and your beautiful children Sasha, Sammy, Gabby and Louis in the UK. Thank you for being my anchor in those years living in London and giving me roots which made it feel like home.

Thank you to all the guests on the *Behind The Mask* podcast and to the incredible creative people who I've humbly and gratefully shared music, theatre and art with in one way or another over the past twenty-plus years. I'd like to make particular mention of Dawson Hann, Nick Evans and the late Tony Scanlon at Wesley College in Melbourne. To all the staff and my classmates at what is now Federation University in Ballarat. To John Foreman AM, Michael Cassel AM, Lord Andrew Lloyd Webber and Sir Cameron Mackintosh for the life-changing opportunities and incredible belief you've shown in me.

To my management team at CMC, in particular James Grierson and Cathy Baker, thank you for your guidance and support, and to David Mann AM, Sam Gance, Radek Sali, Julie Kessel, Marcel Mittelman and Carolyn Jolson for championing me so unconditionally for so many years.

To my teachers, coaches and guides, old, new, alive and passed, for your infinite wisdom and sage advice, in particular Asher Packman, Ben Crowe, Ram Dass and Jonni Pollard (1 Giant Mind). Thank you all for offering me a drawbridge back to my soul and for allowing me to meet and then love the stranger inside myself. In your own ways you have all taught me what true love really is.

This book is here because of all of you. Every one of you has played a part in helping me in some way on this journey through existence. Every interaction, every moment has woven a thread into the tapestry of my life. As Shakespeare said, 'All the world's a stage, and all the men and women merely players.' Thank you all for playing along.

Further reading

Agassi, Andre. *Open: An Autobiography*, HarperCollins, Great Britian, 2010.

Aurelius, Marcus. *Meditations*, Penguin, UK, 2017.

Baird, Julia. *Phosphorescence*, HarperCollins Publishers Australia, Sydney, 2020.

Bly, Robert. *Iron John*, Da Capo Press, UK, 2015.

Brown, Brené. *Daring Greatly: How the Courage to be Vulnerable Transforms the Way We Live, Love, Parent and Lead*, Penguin, UK, 2016.

Byrne, Rhonda. *The Secret*, Simon & Schuster, Great Britian, 2007.

Campbell, Joseph. *The Hero with a Thousand Faces*, New World Library, US, 2012.

Campbell, Joseph. *The Hero's Journey: Joseph Cambell on his Life and Work*, New World Library, 2014.

Cameron, Julia. *The Artist's Way: A Spiritual Path to Higher Creativity*, Profile Books, UK, 2021.

Castaneda Carlos. *The Wheel of Time: The Shamans of Mexico, Their Thoughts about Life, Death and the Universe*, Washington Square, US, 2001.

Coelho, Paulo. *The Alchemist: The 25th Anniversary*, HarperCollins, US, 2015.

Dass, Ram. *Be Here Now*, Random House, US, 1993.

Dass, Ram. *Be Love Now: The Path of the Heart*, HarperOne, US, 2011.

Dass, Ram; Das Rameshwar. *Being Ram Dass*, Sounds True, US, 2023.

Dokic, Jelena. *Fearless: Finding the Power to Thrive*, Penguin Australia, 2023.

His Holiness the Dalai Lama. *The Dalai Lama's Book of Wisdom*, Thorsons/Element, UK, 2000.

His Holiness the Dalai Lama. *The Art of Happiness*, Hachette Australia, Sydney, 2018.

Estés, Clarissa Pinkola. *Women Who Run with the Wolves: Myths and Stories of the Wild Woman Archetype*, Random House UK, 2023.

Ford, Debbie. *The Dark Side of the Light Chasers: Reclaiming Your Power, Creativity, Brilliance, and Dreams*, Hodder & Stoughton, UK, 2001.

Gibran, Khalil. *The Prophet*, Penguin Group USA, UK, 2019.

Gillette, Douglas; Moore, Rober, L. *King, Warrior, Magician, Lover: Rediscovering the Archetypes of the Mature Masculine*, HarperCollins Publishers, US, 1991.

hooks, bell. *All About Love: New Visions*, HarperCollins Publishers, US, 2017.

Jackson, Laura Lynne. *Signs: The Secret Language of the Universe*, Little Brown, UK, 2019.

Jung, C. G. *Modern Man In Search of a Soul*, Taylor & Francis, UK, 2005.

Jung, C. G. *The Archetypes and the Collective Unconscious*, Taylor & Francis, UK, 1991.

Khalili, Nader. *The Spiritual Poems of Rumi*, Quarto, US, 2020.

Holiday, Ryan. *The Obstacle is the Way: The Ancient Art of Turning Adversity to Advantage*, Profile Books, UK, 2015.

Holiday, Ryan; Hanselman, Stephen. *The Daily Stoic: 366 Meditations on Wisdom, Perseverance, and the Art of Living*, Profile Books, UK, 2016.

McConaughey, Matthew. *Greenlights*. Headline, UK, 2023.

Millman, Dan. *The Way of the Peaceful Warrior*, New World Library, US, 2000.

Mitchell, Stephen. *The Bhagavad Gita: A New Translation*, Three Rivers Press, US, 2002.

Osho. *Courage: The Joy of Living Dangerously*, St Martin's Griffin, US, 2011.

Osho. *Love, Feedom, Aloneness*, St Martin's Griffin, US, 2003.

Pollard, Jonni. *The Golden Sequence: A Manual for Reclaiming our Humanity*, BenBella Books, US, 2019.

Rao, Srikumar S. *Modern Wisdom, Ancient Roots: The Movers and Shakers' Guide to Unstoppable Success*, River Grove Books, US, 2022.

Redfield, James. *The Celestine Prophecy*, Bantam Australia, 2011.

Ruiz, Don Miguel. *The Four Agreements: A Practical Guide to Personal Freedom*, Amber Allen, Us, 2011.

Singer, Michael A. *The Surrender Experiment: My Journey into Life's Perfection*, Harmony, US, 2015.

Singer, Michael A. *The Untethered Soul: The Journey Beyond Yourself,* New Harbinger, US, 2007.

Schwartz, Richard C. *No Bad Parts: Healing Trauma and Restoring Wholeness with the Internal Family Systems Model*, Vermillion, US, 2024.

Thusten, Gelong. *Handbook for Hard Time: A Monk's Guide to Fearless Living*, Yellow Kite, UK, 2023.

Tolle, Eckhart. *A New Earth*, Michael Joseph, UK, 2018.

Tolle, Eckhart. *The Power of Now*, New World Library, US, 2004.

Tolle, Eckhart. *Stillness Speaks: Whispers of Now*, Hachette Australia, 2011.

Watts, Alan. *In My Own Way*, New World Library, US, 2007.

Weiss, Brian, L. *Many Lives, Many Masters: The True Story of a Prominent Psychiatrist, His Young Patient, and the Past-Life Therapy That Changed Both Their Lives*, Touchstone, UK, 1988.

Zukav, Gary. *The Seat of the Soul: Inspiring Vision of Humanity's Spiritual Destiny*, Random House UK, 1991.